SPELLS FOR BEGINNERS

2 Books in 1 – Complete Guide to Using Moon Magic, Witchcraft Rituals, and Essential Spells to Improve Your Life

© Copyright 2021 - All rights reserved.

It is not legal to reproduce, duplicate, or transmit any part of this document in either electronic means or in printed format. Recording of this publication is strictly prohibited and any storage of this document is not allowed unless with written permission from the publisher except for the use of brief quotations in a book review.

Disclaimer: Any medicinal benefits given here are a product of my own research and as such should not be taken over the advice of trained medical professionals. Always make sure that anything you consume is 100% safe. If you are pregnant, consult your doctor or midwife before consuming something you haven't tried before.

TABLE OF CONTENTS

Moon Spells for Beginners 16

Introduction 17

Chapter One: Moon Magic Essentials 19

Mother Moon and Her Power and Symbolism 20

Association of Deities With the Power and Energy of the Moon 29

The Moon and the Triple Goddess 35

Creative Pull and Influence of the Moon 38

The Symbolism of the Moon Phases 42

New Moon 42

Crescent Moon 45

Waning Crescent Moon 46

Waxing Crescent Moon 48

First Quarter Moon 50

Gibbous Moon 51

Full Moon 53

Disseminating Moon 57

Last Quarter Moon 59

Balsamic Moon 60

Special Moon Phases 62

Blood Moon 62

Super Moon 64

Frank's Blessed by the Supermoon Water 66

Blue Moon 68

Dark Moon 70

Lunar Eclipse 72

Chapter Two: Moon Spellcasting: 76

Common Tools and Preparation 76

Moon Altars 77

Types of Moon Altars 78

Altar Accessories 79

Preparing for Moon Spells 108

Chapter Three: New Moon Spells 112

New Moon Spells, Rituals, and Ceremonies... 113

Attracting a Lover Spell.. 114

New Romance Spell 115

Facilitating Love Spell.. 117

Fertility Spell... 119

Authenticity Spell 120

Job Hunting Spell... 121

New Moon Divination Spell 123

Adventurous Spell.. 125

Chapter Four: Waxing Crescent Moon Spells for Taking Action... 127

Bathe Me in Confidence Spell............................. 128

Passion Over the Moon Spell.............................. 128

Grant Me Patience Spell 130

I Made the First Move Spell 131

Conflict Resolution Spell 133

Energy Cleansing Ritual 135

Enemy Protection Spell.. 137

Chapter Five: First Quarter Moon Spells for Making Decisions 139

Sacred Water Ritual 140

Healthy Habits Spell 141

Mental Clarity Spell... 143

Make the Right Decision Spell............................ 145

Pivot Spell 147

To Tell the Truth 148

Chapter Six: Waxing Gibbous Moon Spells for Getting Specific 150

Waxing Gibbous Ritual 151

Personification Spell.. 152

Communication Spell 153

Positivity Spell Jar.. 155

Inspirational Moon Spell 157

Reclaim Personal Power Spell 159

Prosperity Spell... 161

Strengthen My Love Spell 163

Chapter Seven: Full Moon Spells for Celebration, Glow, and Reflection.......................... 165

Smoke Cleansing Ritual....................................... 166

Dream Vision Spell... 167

Ritual Steps for Harvesting Full Moon Bliss... 168

Lunar Rejuvenation Spell 169

Self-Love Celebration Spell 171

Chapter Eight: Waning Gibbous Moon Spells for Expressing Gratitude 173

Embracing Obstacles Spell 174

Honor Thy Anger Spell 175

Honoring a Relationship Spell 176

Thanksgiving Ritual During Waning Gibbous Moon 177

Minimalism Moon Spell 178

Thanking Mother Earth Spell 179

Chapter Nine: Waning Crescent Moon for Surrender and Release 182

Dark Goddess Ritual 183

Banish My Alcohol Addiction Spell 185

You Need to Cut the Cord Spell 186

Final Thoughts 190

References 192

Wicca Spell Book for Beginners 195

Introduction 197

Chapter One: Witchcraft Rituals 201

    Intention 201

    Candle Magic 209

    Opening and Closing a Circle Ritual 213

    Creating your Altar 215

    Runes Ritual 217

Chapter Two: White Magic Spells 220

    Crystal Magic 220

    Essential Oils and Magic 222

    Types of Magical Essential Oils 223

    Essential Herbs and Magic 225

    Magical Herbs 227

    Frank's "Moon-Blessed Water" Recipe 230

    Frank's Healing Spell to Keep you Safe and Sound (Basic Healing Spell) 231

    "Peaceful Mind" Spell (for Calming) 235

    Bathing Spells for Spiritual Cleansing and Protection 236

"Much-Needed Sleep" Spell 239

Black Salt Recipe 242

"Protect Your Home" Spell 243

Home Protection Crystal Enchantment Spell . 244

"Children Need Protection" Spell 246

Prosperity Spells 248

"Money Grows on Trees" Spell.......................... 249

"Money Over the Moon" Spell........................... 250

"Witch's Bottle" Spell to Sell............................... 251

Garden Growth Elemental Spell 252

"Rain Dance" Spell 255

"Rain, Rain Go Away" Storm Protection
Spell.. 255

"Confidence in Me" Tea 257

Goal Accomplishment Jar Spell 259

"Communication is a Two-Way Street" Spell 260

"New Love Spell" for Blessing a
Relationship 262

"Mend a Broken Heart" Spell.............................. 263

Aphrodite Beauty Oil.. 265

Black Obsidian and Clear Quartz Protection Stone Duo 266

Protection Jar Spell 267

Banish the Dark Spells 270

Banish by Burning 271

Banish by Candle 272

"There's the Door" Spell for Banishing a Toxic Person from Your Life 273

"Sacred Cleansing Water" Recipe 274

"Removing Evil from an Object" Spell 275

Banishing Sigil 276

"Walk Away your Troubles" Spell 278

Ancestral Communion Spell 278

"I Need Closure" Spell 281

Sea Sage Cleansing 283

Invocation of Hecate 284

Invocation of Nyx 287

Bonding with a Familiar 289

Choosing your Familiar 290

How to Call a Familiar 290

Chapter Three: Red Magic Spells Hoodoo 293

What is Hoodoo/Folk Magic............................. 293

"Love Bell" Spell... 295

"Love Knot" Spell.. 297

Love Potion #9 Passion Tea Aphrodisiac........ 299

"Bathing in Sensuality" Aphrodisiac Spell 301

Candle Carving Ritual (Scribing)...................... 303

"Letting Go of a Lover" Spell 306

Aphrodite Sea Charm 308

"Adoration Candle" Spell 310

Hathor's Bath Ritual.. 311

Birch Bark Love Spell.. 312

Reverse Love Spell... 314

Attraction Poppet 315

Chapter Four: Sorcery/Hex Spells........................ 318

Ceremonial Magic 319

Left and Right Hand Magic 320

Protection Spell 320

Rune of Protection 321

Pepper Pentacle.. 323

"Summon a Storm" Spell 326

Casting A Shadow Circle 327

Summoning Succubae's Lament 328

Invocation of Lyssa 329

Liar's Lamentation Spell 330

A Seduction Spell 331

"Tattered Hearts" Spell Part I 333

"Tattered Hearts" Spell Part II 334

Carman's Hex 335

Binding by Fear 335

Spell to Bind a Bully 336

Spell for Stopping Harassment 338

Sour Jar 339

Discord and Darkness Spell 340

Bad Luck Potion 341

"Ring of Power" Enchantment 342

Effigy Poppet Curse 343

"Nightmare Jar" Spell 344

"Banishing Your Ex" Hex 346

"You're so Vain and Insane" Hex 347

Business Butcher Curse 348

Poppet Curse of Slight Pain 349

"Agony of Acne" Curse 350

"Evil Eye" Enchantment 350

Steps to Ward Off the Evil Eye 351

Chapter Five: Rune Casting & Divination 353

TIWAZ (Tyr) 354

BERKANO (Birch Goddess) 355

EHWAZ (Horse) 356

MANNAZ (Mankind) 357

LAGUZ (Water) 358

INGWAZ or INGUZ (Seed) 359

DAGAZ (Dawn) 360

RAIDHO (Riding) 361

KENAZ (Torch) 362

GEBO (Gift) 363

WUNJO (Joy) 364

HAGALAZ (Hail) 365

NAUTHIZ (Necessity) 366

ISA (Ice) 367

ANSUZ (Speech) 368

THURISAZ (Thorn) 369
OTHALA (Homeland) 370
JERA (Year) 371
EIHWAZ or IHWAZ (Yew Tree) 372
PERTHRO (Unknown) 374
ALGIZ (Life) 375
SOWILO (Sun) 376
FEHU (Cattle) 377
URUZ (AUROCHS) 379
Three Norns Method 380
Scrying 381
Water Scrying Method 384
Pendulum Dowsing 386
How Pendulum Dowsing Works 387
The Futhark Runes 390

Final Thoughts 393
Sources 397

SPECIAL BONUS!

Thank you for adding this book to your Wiccan Library! To learn more, join Frank's Wiccan Community and get this additional free *Wicca Starter Kit* book 100% FREE!

If you want insider access plus this Free Wicca Starter Kit Book, all you have to do is **scan the code below** with your smartphone camera to claim your offer!

MOON SPELLS FOR BEGINNERS

Your Complete Guide to the Hidden Power of Lunar Phases, Wiccan Magic, Rituals, and Witchcraft

Frank Bawdoe

INTRODUCTION

It is no secret that witches love Mother Moon and that learning how to harness lunar powers can amplify your magic and help you manifest amazing spells. Witches and non-witches alike, most of us feel a connection to the moon. For Wiccans, the moon represents the mother or feminine energy, and the sun represents the father or masculine energy. I remember being in elementary school and feeling a great sense of comfort in the moon and being amazed that it was so present, yet so far away.

Almost every culture has deities corresponding with our Moon, which should come as no surprise since the Moon's position in the sky heralds the change in seasons. The word lunar is derived from the Latin word *Luna*, which is feminine. The Moon has influenced human behavior since the start of humankind. Unlike the Sun, the Moon has a differential pull, meaning that its gravitational pull on the Earth is strongest on the side facing the moon.

This is what causes the tides. Two-thirds of the human body is water, so if the moon can shift the waters in the oceans, it can certainly influence the fluids and chemicals in our body, affecting behavior. Moon magic is undoubtedly one of Nature's greatest forces and assists Wiccans and non-witches in using lunar energy to practice magic. For Wiccans, the magic of the Moon provides a more powerful connection with the Goddess and all that she has in store for you. The moon not only charges your crystals, candles, oils, and herbs, it charges you!

I am looking forward to you gaining a deep understanding of the fundamentals of Moon magic and its many manifestations through reading this book. We will discuss how the moon's phases affect magic, how to utilize lunar magic in everyday living, how the Moon corresponds with the Triple Goddess, what special moons are, and tools you'll need for Moon magic. I have provided you with several rituals and spells for you to perform for each phase of the moon, and so much more. Even if you are new to Moon magic, this book will give you all of the necessary background, traditions, and tools you need to start practicing lunar magic right now.

CHAPTER 1:

MOON MAGIC ESSENTIALS

I have been practicing moon magic to clear away negativity and to manifest my intentions for more than a decade. I often use the full Moon and new Moon when I am self-reflecting on what areas in my life I want to change, and what I want to experience more of. Moon veneration, worship, adoration, Moon deities, and symbolic representation of the Moon have been connected with the vibrational energies of the Universe and the rhythms of life. The sacredness of the moon—and the widespread phenomenon with which it is associated—has appeared in various cultures and eras throughout documented history. It is richly engrained in mythology and symbolism.

Lunar magic is seen in terms of the vibrational energy of the cosmos and is thought to govern the processes of all change vital to life. The cycles of the Moon's appearance and disappearance is the foundation for the widely known connection between the Moon and the land of the dead, the region souls travel to after death, and the power to be reborn. Likewise, the Moon's governance over the cycle of life associates the moon with fate.

Mother Moon and Her Power and Symbolism

The lunar phases represent immortality, eternity, and the dark side or enlightenment of Mother Nature. The Moon is a reflection of humankind's inner wisdom or the phases of human life on earth. As previously mentioned, the moon controls the season, tides, rains, and waters. It falls somewhere between the light of the day and the darkness of the night, and therefore is associated with the realm between the unconscious and the conscious. In astrology, the moon symbolizes the soul; in horoscopes, it mandates the person's ability for adaptation and reflection. It gives an analogy of the developmental stages of human life: infancy corresponds with the new moon, adolescence with the crescent moon, maturity with the full moon, and sleep or life's decline with the waning moon. Just the sight of the moon in the night's sky practically forces us to take pause and stand in awe.

Watching the moon during the night is mesmerizing, and when it is full, we are charmed by its grandiosity. It takes some effort to pause and notice when the Moon is barely visible, and we tend to forget about it until we learn that every shape and form it takes has meaning. One really interesting correspondence with the full Moon is the specific names it's given according to the month it falls on. It is important to cultivate an intimate relationship with Mother Moon, especially for witches. The more you know her, the more cosmic energy you can harness. For instance, every full moon has a name, but occasionally there are more than twelve full moons in a year. For instance, the full moon in August is called the Sturgeon Moon because it is the best time of the year to catch sturgeon fish, and a second full Moon in August is called the Red Moon because it appears reddish due to the light fighting its way through the Summer horizon.

Different cultures have given names to full Moons across the lunar calendar. Many of the Moon's nicknames have come to us from Native American culture because of their lifestyle, the cycles of the lunar phases were just as important a method of timekeeping as the longer solar cycle of the year, from which the modern method is derived.

The cycle repeats itself, symbolizing the Earth's natural processes and life's natural cycles happening with us and to us. The Moon dictates what happens on Earth, including our emotions and the ocean's tides. It affects animal behavior as well as human behavior, which is why—even in its most subtle form—it is a powerful symbol of influence. The phases of the Moon don't quite line up with the modern-day calendar or Gregorian calendar. Every so often, there is more than one full Moon in a month, and the second Moon is called a blue moon or a red moon.

Symbols of the Moon also include:
- Mystery
- Transition
- Renewal
- Rebirth
- Darkness
- Emotion
- Time

The Moon Represents:

1. *The Natural Cycle*

    The Moon is constantly changing depending on where it is situated relative to the Sun and the Earth, which is why it's more visible some nights than others. Everything in life, just like the Moon, has its own cycle. It's like how people wake up every morning, go to school or work, come home, make dinner, watch TV, read a book, take a shower, go to bed, and get up the next morning to repeat the cycle. This ongoing cycle is what keeps us ticking.

The Moon phases also represent growth and decline. We start out young and full of energy, and then we reach our apex, symbolized by the full Moon's brightness. As we age, our energy levels drop, and our strength lessens like the cycle of the moon.

2. *Femininity*

The Moon is associated with feminine energy and, with the Sun, can be seen in the symbol yin and yang. Usually, the moon is connected to feminine characteristics, such as delicacy and passion. The yin and yang display the characteristics of the polarity of the Sun and Moon. The Moon is darker and cold; the Sun is bright and hot. They portray polar opposites, which is why the Moon corresponds with yin and the Sun with yang.

The Moon's cycle is around 28 days, the same as a woman's menstrual cycle. This is one of the reasons that the moon was considered female to the ancient people because it had a cycle like that of a female. For the Hellenic polytheists and the Wiccans, the Moon Mother is gentle, beautiful, kind, and nurturing. The full Moon symbolized the big round pregnant belly.

The Moon goddess, Changi, has been worshiped since ancient times by followers of the traditional Chinese religions. Changi bore twelve moons, while Xihe, one of her husband's other wives, bore ten suns. These two lunar goddesses, together symbolize yin and yang, as well as the Chinese lunar and solar calendars.

3. *Subconscious*

   While sleeping, humans don't exactly know what is going on around them. The night is always full of mysteries and secrets, which connect to us without our knowledge, specifically to our subconscious dreams and thoughts. The Moon is behind the scenes, doing its job while we sleep. The phase of the moon directly affects our moods as it controls much of our fluid fluctuations. After all, almost three-fourths of our brain is made up of water.

4. *Influence*

Without our knowledge, the Moon influences our behaviors. For instance, a full moon can bring about overly emotional or irritated feelings, or a sudden sense of increased energy. For others, the full Moon can bring about angry and sleeping feelings. Some animals become much more active during a full Moon. It affects all things, because if one thing is influenced, there is a change that ripples through all things. This is known as the butterfly effect.

As such, the moon has an effect on us and everything around us, making it a powerful yet somewhat hidden influence on planet Earth.

5. *Darkness*

Since the moon is present at night time, it symbolizes darkness in a way that connects us to the darkness. The less full the Moon is, the darker it is. But, even when it is full, it is still dark outside. For many, this is a peaceful serenity, and for others, it is scary. Also, without thinking, we see the Moon as darkness because we compare it to the Sun. Witches are often comfortable on the darker side of this duality, but with all things balance is key. The Moon can also be associated with the darker side of our personality; the part of us that stays hidden, and like the moon, tends to reveal itself at night.

6. *Mystery*

   The Moon and the stars carry a mysterious element. In ancient times, up until only about fifty years ago, the Moon was unexplored, even though it seemed so very close to us. It wasn't until Galileo, in 1609, did humans start to take more of an interest in the Moon as an entity. It wasn't until then did humans know, by way of the telescope, that the Moon has valleys, mountains, and other characteristics similar to the Earth.

7. *Emotion*

   The Moon is often thought of as what governs human emotions, and that people are deeply affected by the size of the Moon. When full, it brings about strong emotions, as previously mentioned is obvious by its effects on animals.

   a. *Full Moon*: When the Moon is intense, like when it is full, anxiety levels can rise, and people can even feel a bit manic. The full Moon has also been documented to intensify nightmares and dreams, which can have an impact on the following day's emotions (Fellizar & Kahn, 2021).

b. *New Moon*: When there is a new moon, people tend to self-examine or delve into natural introspection. We can't see the moon when it is new, so its available energy levels are lower. People tend to report feeling more fatigued, causing them to naturally turn to their inner thoughts. Witches can take full advantage of the new Moon's cosmic energy to set their intentions and figure out what they want out of life. The new Moon starts a fresh lunar cycle, so its energy naturally supports new beginnings (Kahn, 2020). The first half of the lunar cycle is a time for setting intentions and goals for spell crafting. Witchcraft during the first half of the lunar cycle is a good idea because as the moon grows—known as waxing—so do motivations and energies. This is a time to take on new projects, during this two-week period where the new moon is developing into a full moon.

c. *Waxing Moon*: During the waxing moon, sleep disturbances can occur, which makes sense because as the moon grows, there is an increased energy because we can see and do more. Several studies on the subject indicate that sleep is significantly affected by the waxing phase of the Moon (Cajochen, et al., 2013).

d. *Waning Moon*: This is the phase where the Moon's illuminated section is decreasing, slowing us down and giving us a sense of letting go, cleansing, and releasing. This is a good time to let go of any resentments and regrets. It's a time for forgiveness and purging what no longer has a purpose. It is time to donate your old clothes, throw away old makeup, and to get rid of anything weighing you down. Refresh your altar, sweep your doorways, and prepare for upcoming magic.

8. *Renewal*

Each night we renew ourselves by sleeping, which is also the time when the Moon shines. Also, the Moon symbolizes the soul's renewal through reincarnation. Humans are born, grow into mature adults, continue to age, then eventually die, and the children's birth starts the cycle all over again. The concept of renewal or rebirth can be found in almost every religion or belief system and has been around since ancient mythology. Pagan religions, including Wicca, do not have such a direct concept of rebirth but instead believe in nature's elements, such as the Moon, Sun, water, and trees, which are continuously reborn and regenerated. For Wiccans and pagans alike, the rebirth symbols are also associated with mental, physical, and spiritual renewal.

9. *Eternity*

   The Moon has been always there, even before humans gazed upon it. It is always somewhere out on the horizon. Because it always has been and always will be; it remains a symbol of immortality and eternity.

Association of Deities With the Power and Energy of the Moon

For millennia, humans have gazed up at the Moon and wondered about its association with deities and its divine significance. Most cultures throughout history have had gods and goddesses associated with the energy and powers of the Moon. In Wiccan and pagan rituals, lunar deities can be called upon for assistance.

Common Deities Across Various Cultures

1. *Alignak/Igaluk* (Inuit): For the ancient Inuit peoples, Alignak is both the Moon god and the weather god. He governs eclipses and earthquakes and controls the tides. Legend has it that he is responsible for carrying the souls of the dead back to Earth for rebirth. He is the protector of fishermen from the wrath of the sea goddess, Sedna. It is said that Alignak committed incest with his sister and was banned from the Earth. His sister, Malina, became the Sun goddess and Alignak the Moon god. It is said that the two reunite during the solar eclipse.
2. *Artemis* (Greek): Artemis is the goddess of the hunt. She is the twin sister of Apollo, who is a Sun god. She is portrayed in artwork of the post-Classical period as always being beside a crescent moon. She is also the goddess of purity, nature, and childbirth. She was the daughter of Leto and Zeus and became the goddess of wild things and the wilderness. Artemis in her Roman form is Diana. She is queen of the Moon and brings forth good luck. If you can't find something, invoke the goddess Artemis, and she will help you find it.

Artemis, the lunar goddess, can illuminate your life, your magic, and your spells.

3. *Cerridwen* (Celtic): In ancient Celtic legend, Cerridwen is the keeper of the cauldron that holds within it all knowledge. She is the giver of inspiration and wisdom. As a Moon goddess, she corresponds with intuitiveness. She is known by the full Moon and often represented as a white sow, symbolizing fertility, maternity, and fecundity. She is the Crone and the Mother.

4. *Chang'e* (Chinese): In ancient Chinese legend, Chang'e is the Moon goddess. She was married to a great archer, King Hou Ti. But he became tyrannical and spread destruction and death all over his land. He treated his people with brutality and starved them. He greatly feared dying and went to a healer who gave him a magic potion that allowed him to become immortal. But Chang'e stole his elixir while he lay sleeping, so he could not live forever, for that would have been a terrible thing. King Hou Yi went after Chang'e and demanded she give him back the potion. She drank it immediately and flew up into the sky, becoming the Moon. Chinese mythology cites this as an example of self-sacrifice for the best interest of others.

5. *Coyolxauhqui* (Aztec): Ancient Aztec folklore tells the story of Coyolxauhqui, the sister to Huitzilopochtli, an Aztec god. She was killed, along with all of her siblings, when her brother leaped from their mother's womb. Huitzilopochtli decapitated Coyolxauhqui and threw her head up into the sky, where it became the Moon. She is portrayed in Aztec artwork as beautiful young woman, adorned with lunar symbols and decorated with bells.
6. *Hecate* (Greek): The Dark Goddess, Hecate is associated with the dark moon, magic, and the spirit world. She is the goddess of ghosts. In ancient Greek poetry, when Hecate was born of Artemis and Apollo, Phoebe, a lunar goddess reappeared during the moon's darkest phase. Hecate banishes evil and is the goddess of the intersection of the three paths. Invoking Hecate helps bring things to an end. She is there for funeral ceremonies, remembrance, and rites of passage to the other world. She personifies the prophecy circle of the dark moon and should be invited when in need of great insight and wisdom. Perform a dark moon ritual with Hecate for fresh starts and to gain ultimate feminine foresight.

7. *Selene* (Greek): Selene is a herald in Greek mythology, as she was praised and worshiped during the full moon. She had a young lover, a shepherd named Prince Endymion. Zeus granted him immortality; however his immortality was to be spent in a cave, sleeping forever. Out of her love for him, Selene came down every night from the sky to sleep next to him. Early classical Greek poets depict her as the moon incarnate. Selene cast light on to the Earth, and therefore on all living things, inside and out. She is the teacher of all things magic and supernatural through passing on her gifts of intelligence and special knowledge, granting those you invoke her the ability to have clarity.

8. *Hina/Sina* (Polynesian): One of the most well-known Polynesian lunar deities is Hina, or Sina, who lives within the moon itself. She is the protector of night travelers. According to ancient Hawwiian legend, Sina once lived on the Earth but grew tired of the way her family and husband treated her, so she packed up all of her things and went to live on the Moon. Tahitian folklore tells the story that Sina was curious and wanted to explore the Moon, so she paddled her magic canoe and flew to the Moon. Once she arrived, she

fell in love with the Moon's tranquility and beauty and quickly decided she never wanted to leave. She is the oldest known goddess and is associated with feminine energy (wahine). Hina is known for her healing properties and is portrayed as Maui's wife, sister, mother, or grandmother. Hina watched over childbirth, and female babies were often dedicated to her.

9. *Thoth* (Egyptian): Ancient Egyptian lore holds Thoth to be the moon god of wisdom and magic. In some Egyptian legends, Thoth is said to weigh the souls of the dead. In ancient Egyptian artwork, Thoth is portrayed with a crescent on his head. Invoking Thoth brings forth the workings of fate, wisdom, and magic. He is the one to involve when you write your Book of Shadows, a spell, or cast words of healing. You can also invoke Thoth to help you mediate a dispute. He was one of the most important Egyptian lunar deities and was said to be self-created, and therefore also became the god of equilibrium, corresponding to both chaos and order.

The Moon and the Triple Goddess

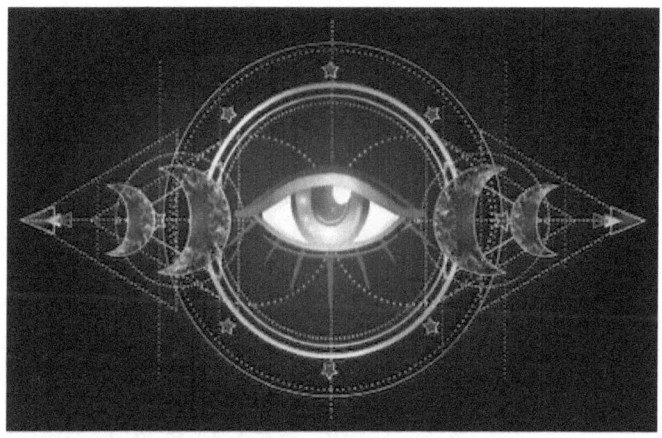

The Triple Goddess, who is revered in Neopagan religious and rituals, represents the trinity of the Maiden, the Mother, and the Crone—a three-fold form depicting the phases of female maturity and are also aligned with the Moon's phases as it orbits around the Earth. The waxing crescent, the full moon, and the waning crescent. But while all females move linearly through each of the phases during her lifetime, each of the Triple Goddess's aspects has characteristics that resonate in all of us, both female and male, at varying times in our lives. The Triple Goddess also reflects upon the complexities of the human mind—spiritual, mental, emotional—as well as the cycle of life that Earthlings experience.

Each of the Triple Goddess's aspects corresponds with specific seasons, the natural elements, human characteristics, and other naturalistic phenomena. These correspondences can be used to involve the most suitable aspect of the Triple Goddess for ritual ceremonies, spellcasting, prayer, and worship.

The Waxing Moon and the Maiden

The Maiden aspect of the Triple Goddess represents the youthful stage of a female's life and aligns with the crescent-to-waxing phase of the Moon. The waxing moon represents a period of growth, as it transforms into fullness. These phases of the Moon are reflected by the Maiden in the cycles of nature and correspond with the Spring season, dawn, and sunrise. The Maiden is also known as the Virgin or the Huntress. Her correspondence with Spring portrays her as innocent and young. When there is a waxing moon, invoking the Maiden or Persephone, Artemis, Rhiannon, or Freya works for any type of new beginning, such as new love, new employment, a new home, a new baby, etc. White is the symbolized color for the Maiden, who shows her face while the Moon is waxing. She is associated with innocence, independence, youth, self-confidence, self-discovery, exploration, intelligence, and creativity.

The Full Moon and the Mother

When the moon becomes full, the Maiden transforms to the Mother, giving birth to bountiful riches to all on Earth. She represents Summer and midday, the greenest time of the year with flowers and forests flourishing—and animals growing from youth to maturity. For humans, she is associated with adulthood, nurturing, responsibility, and the fullness that life has to offer. The Mother, as the full moon, is considered by witches to be the most powerful aspect of the Triple Goddess. The Mother Goddess was the inspiration for Gardnerian Wicca's understanding of the divine feminine. Invoking Demeter, Selene, Ceres, Danu, or Badb as the Mother Goddess in lunar magic is best for marriage, big decisions, fertility, and childbirth.

The Waning Moon and the Crone

The nights grow darker as the Moon wanes, and the Crone assumes her position of power. Also known as the Hag, she is associated with the later years of life, specifically post menopausal. She corresponds with Winter and Autumn, night, sunset, and the end of the growing season. She is the wisest aspect of the Triple Goddess, and governs past lives, aging, visions, death and rebirth, prophecy, transformations, and guidance. She was feared as an entity for thousands of years because she reminds us that death is a part of life, just as the dark phase of the

Moon introduces the new moon. The Hag or Crone goddess is associated with the underworld and death. Invoking the dark Goddess Hecate, Baba Yaga, Morrigan, or Cailleach Bear should be used for magic, sorcery, ghosts, and the spirit world.

The aspects of the Triple Goddess are indeed a complex and diverse declaration of the divine feminine. For Wiccans and pagans who worship her, she provides constant opportunities to grow and learn through aligning with her three aspects. Making a conscious effort to align your adoration with the phases of the Moon will provide you with a more rewarding and an even deeper spiritual connection with the Triple Goddess.

Creative Pull and Influence of the Moon

Traditional Wiccan approaches to rituals and magic respect the principles of sympathetic magic. Sympathetic magic dictates the timing of ceremonial magic, and rituals should align with the energetic shifts of the Earth when possible. The influence of the Moon's cosmic energies cannot be denied, as we continuously bear witness to its creative pull in the changing tides, our behavior, subconscious or dreams, and the cycles of the human body. Synchronizing our lives with the Moon's phases can help us live in greater harmony with nature, its elements, and its ever-changing seasons.

Mother Moon is the celestial neighbor that lives closest to us. Even though in size, it is much smaller than our other celestial friend, the Sun. When it comes to gravitational pull, our Moon, be it a small satellite, expends two and a half times the gravitational force of the sun (Dragonsong, 2021). The Moon governs five tides, each of which are vital in the Earth's capabilities of supporting life. To Wiccans and other pagan religions, the Moon corresponds to the female facet of divinity and embodies the characteristics of Yin—which include fluidity, eternity, ever-changing, and life-bearing. Mother moon provides a soft light that guides us through life's many mysteries.

The creative influence of the Moon and the important aspects of life she affects include five primary Wiccan paradoxes and processes:
1. Chaos and Mystery
2. Evolutionary flow
3. Birth & Death
4. Soul and Emotions
5. Magic and Wisdom

The documented influences of the Full Moon include:

- Triggers breeding cycles and life's natural rhythms.
- Marks ovulation periods in humans and herbivores.
- Peak deer mating season happens during two full moons.
- Annually, the water temperature and cues from the lunar cycle encourage whole coral reef colonies to release their sperm and tiny eggs (gametes) into the ocean. It appears as a beautiful underwater blizzard of cascading colorful flakes by the billions in orange, yellow, red, and white.
- Birds appear to migrate by following the Moon's patterns to find their path of migration.

- During the Hunter's Moon, also known as the blood moon, game birds return to specific locations, usually in the month of October.
- During the full moon, salmon and bears move. Also called the Full Moon Salmon Mover, which lures the bears to feed, thus putting them on the move.
- More animal injuries are reported during a full moon. Studies documented a 28 percent increase in dog visits to the veterinarian emergency room and a 23 percent increase in cat visits (Poppick, 2013).
- Studies indicated that oysters have a lunar rhythm for when they open their shells to spawn and eat. They tend to be significantly more closed during a full moon, and tend to spawn and eat during new moons (Daley, 2019).
- There is a 15 percent rise in automobile accidents due to the Werewolf Effect (McDermott, 2019). McDermott and his colleagues (2019) theorized that the moon's intensity tends to excite drivers, and they become more easily distracted after a study of 850,000 accidents.

- Electrical charges in all living cells are amplified by the full moon (Andrews, 2018).

The Symbolism of the Moon Phases

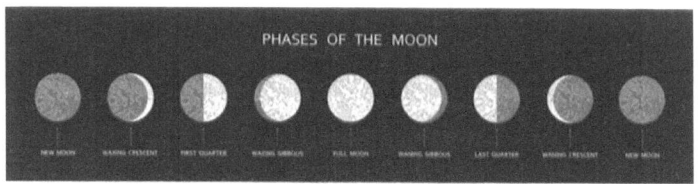

The phases of the Moon are so influential they can even be seen among the most popular tattoo designs. The Moon signifies spirituality and provides us with a feeling of connectedness to all that is cosmic energy. The Moon phases are just like a seed that grows into a seedling, then blossoms into a flower, and then dies. Once you learn to align yourself with the Moon, you can activate her natural powers and draw into yourself her innate characteristics of creativity, change, femininity, and fluidity. Male witches need to learn how to harness the powers of femininity just as much as female witches.

New Moon

The beginning of the lunar phases is dark and represents fresh beginnings or turning over a new leaf. It's time to pick ourselves up, set goals for the future, and plan for achievement over the next moon phase. Once a month, a new Moon happens when it conjoins in the sky with the sun. We can't see a new moon at first, but then it appears slowly, first as a very thin, illuminated crescent. Even though it is thought to last for three days, a new moon is only new for a moment, when the Moon and the Sun are in direct alignment in the sky. The new moon signifies the beginning of a cycle and can be thought of as a cosmic energy reset. It is prime time for goal setting and developing your intentions to manifest as the moon waxes into fullness. Aligning with the Moon's energies can help to give you a good sense of direction and grounding.

New Moon

Magical Practices for a New Moon:
1. Set an intention that is worthwhile. Each month the new moon offers up some extra intention-setting magic, so focus on those things you are specifically passionate about. Make sure your intentions are clear, specific, and concise as you can make them. You want to let the universe know your goals and aspirations during your New Moon Ritual.
2. Have a candle lighting ceremony. It is the darkest night of the whole month, so candles burn bright. Ask the Moon to illuminate you during this phase and all the phases to follow. Make sure your candle is charged and in a safe spot to burn through the night.
3. Start something new. The Moon is most fertile when it is new. Apply for that job you have been wanting, learn a new language, most of all do something novel.
4. Write a new moon wish list. Write down the details of your wishes. If you wish for new furniture, describe its color, shape, and size. Picture an image of your wants and focus on what it means to you.
5. Create a sacred moon altar for holding your moon-blessed objects and water.

What to Avoid During a New Moon

1. Quitting a situation or leaving person you care about. Use your energy to start something new rather than end something.
2. Not meeting new people. Don't miss out on the lessons and possibilities of new friendships or love interests.
3. Declining invitations. Get up and go, a new moon is the perfect time for accepting random invitations to anything,
4. Spending time with exhausting people—energy suckers.

Crescent Moon

The crescent moon represents femininity, growth, and thriving. Many years ago, it was thought to be symbolic of acquisition or conquest, but witch-hunters considered it to be a threat, so they would light a symbolic representation on fire in the land where a witch lived to let them know they were marked. The crescent moon is considered sacred to Wiccans, as it is associated with feminine power, psychic visions, the divine feminine, and creation.

Crescent Moon

Waning Crescent Moon

When the crescent moon is waning, its magic is used to banish negative or evil energies that are within a situation or a person. It is also worshiped when its magic is needed to remove hexes, end a relationship, break a spell, and help us to remember important things while starting on a fresh beginning. When the crescent moon is waning, it is referring to endings, doors closing, relationships ending, and previously casted spells ending. It is sometimes showing you to let go of something you no longer need but are still trying to hold onto. Use waning crescent moon magic for closing the doors on bad health, bad luck, and bad relationships! It symbolizes lessening—a lesser or lower state of movement and power. It is a time to compartmentalize and give in to feelings of sadness so you can let it go. The waning crescent moon represents the passing of time.

Waning Crescent Moon

Magic Acts for the Waning Crescent Moon:

- Removing negativity
- Breaking hexes and curses
- Cleansing objects and other people
- Cleansing rituals for your home and yourself
- Ending a love spell that has been placed on you
- Ridding yourself of negative personality characteristics and bad habits (addictions, etc.)

- Ridding yourself of your enemies once and for all
- Releasing pent up anger or rage
- Clearing the clutter from your mind

Waxing Crescent Moon

When the crescent moon is waxing, it symbolizes those new beginnings, gearing you up for the start of new projects or when you want to bring new things into your life. As the Moon heads toward fullness, your energy level will increase, providing you with the strength you need to complete your projects. It is a time to plan for the future, make wishes, and realize your hopes. It is a time to declare our desires for the new lunar month and hope for the best.

Waxing Crescent Moon

Intention Spell for Waxing Crescent Moon

1. On the first day of the waxing crescent moon, go outside.
2. Write your intention with a sharpie on a bay leaf and hold it between your palms.
3. Express your gratitude to the waxing crescent moon for coming to your ritual by holding your hands toward the moon and saying thank you aloud.
4. When you start feeling the vibrational energy of the waxing crescent moon, pull your hands with the bay leaf toward your heart.
5. Meditate on your intention and visualize it as if it has already manifested.
6. Light your bay leaf on fire and let it burn completely in an abalone shell.
7. Watch the smoke and ashes of the bay leaf float up toward the moon.
8. Trust that your intention was received by the Moon and know it has already started to manifest.
9. Thank the moon and complete your spell.

First Quarter Moon

The first quarter moon represents the importance of having a head start for facing and conquering the challenges you were not prepared for, it is also the symbol for the time to make impulsive decisions and act. It is the best time for conducting magic to draw things in, such as money, love, success, good health, and a productive time for calling back lost objects. The first quarter moon is a time to acknowledge any obstacles in your way, keeping you from getting your needs met. It is a time to focus on unblocking and aligning your chakras, taking spiritual baths, lighting candles, and maybe trying some nature-oriented exercise. The first quarter moon magic is great for success, abundance, and love. It is time for hard work and action with the arrival of the first quarter moon. It is a time to be prepared and flexible to make important decisions when things don't go as planned. Try a new recipe or cast your favorite attraction spell. The best time to cast a love spell is during the first quarter moon, and if you can do it on a Friday and a first quarter moon, it will have double the manifesting power. Remember, Friday is Venus Day.

First Quarter Moon

Gibbous Moon

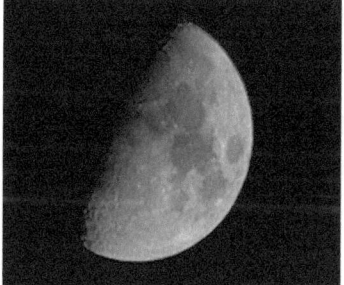

Waning Gibbous Moon   Waxing Gibbous Moon

Waning Gibbous Moon

The waning gibbous moon phase is between the full moon phase and the previous quarter moon phase. The word waning means diminishing. It looks not quite full, but a bit more than half illuminated. It rises later in the night than the full moon. You can usually see it in the early morning hours, and it is quite spiritual. Sometimes, you can catch an eerie glimpse of it looking like a misshapen, glowing red moon when it is close to the horizon. This is an important time to think about what you have pent up and need to release. Consider anything blocking you from achieving your desired outcomes. Your energy levels may be slowing down, but also leaving you feeling satiated and grateful. To make the most of this phase of the Moon, make a gratitude journal and use it for all of the phases. This is a perfect phase of the Moon for sharing the love, taking a friend out for lunch, reconnecting with old friends, and apologizing to anyone you snapped at during a full moon.

Waxing Gibbous Moon

The waxing gibbous moon is much like the waxing crescent moon, but when the gibbous moon is waxing, the illuminated section of the Moon is increasing, to eventually become a full moon. During the waxing gibbous moon phase, you can be facing some challenges. It is a good time to practice patience. Do your best to stay flexible and take a moment to jot down things you are grateful for. Pay close attention to your inner-being and trust in yourself. The waxing gibbous moon phase is an opportune time for consulting the Runes or Tarot cards. It is the time for evaluation, taking a step back, and looking closely at your life. What are we doing right? What are we doing wrong? If you want answers to those questions, simply ask the waxing gibbous moon! Correct your actions if needed and adapt to your current situation. During the waxing gibbous moon phase, it is a good time to improve and refine the intentions you set during the new moon.

Full Moon

The beautiful, big, and bright full moon is the most iconic, notorious, and spectacular moment of the lunar cycle. The full moon is both figuratively and literally a time of illumination and culmination that can help us realize the fruits of our labor, bring energy levels to a head, and see things with more clarity. Often associated with howling wolves, intensity, and chaos, the full moon has earned its reputation. Because the full moon is the biggest and brightest moment of the lunar cycle, it brings energy that is just as extreme. Full moons can turn the quietest of individuals into social butterflies, but take caution not to wear yourself out. The full moon is quite literally your cosmic guidance counselor.

In the full moon phase, the Moon, Sun, and the Earth are in perfect alignment. Differing from the new moon phase, the full moon is on the opposite side of the Earth, so we see the side that the Sun is shining on. The Moon and the Sun are opposing signs on the zodiac, so you may feel some frustration and a bit of tension as the opposing energies are pulling on you. To make the most of the full moon phase, embrace your added energy and channel it into activities and projects you feel passionate about. This is the time to realize and manifest the intentions you set for your magic during the other phases of the Moon. It is the time for the completion of objectives you set and reach the peak of your prowess! It is also a symbol of power and purity. The full moon is a master charger, so set your vases, cauldrons, kettles, and anything else that can hold water outside under the full moon. I put mine on top of my car at nightfall and bring it in at dawn. I used the moon-blessed water for drinking, putting into my pet's bowl, watering my plants, infusing essential oils, added to my bath, anointing candles, charging my crystals, you name it, Moon-blessed water is capable of powerful magic.

Full Moon

When the Moon was in its new phase, it was a good time for goal setting and starting new projects, but full moons are more about putting things into motion and finishing those projects. The full moon is also associated with shedding or releasing any toxic patterns or habits in your life.

Full Moon Ritual

1. Ground yourself: Find a comfortable place to sit and commune with the full moon. Ask Mother Moon to help you be present in the moment with her there to ground you.

2. Tune into Mother Moon and Mother Nature: Surrounding yourself with nature has a grounding and calming effect. Charging up your call to nature during a full moon can help to quell your anxiety and bring clarity to any unanswered questions. Being one with the full moon and nature is healing and will align your body with its natural rhythms. Take a nature walk or bathe in the forest.
3. Mediate with Mother Moon
4. Journal under the full moonlight: Even if you are just writing a description of how the Moon is making you feel.
5. Write your spells and charge them with the full moon. Leave your Book of Shadows on a table or rooftop under a full moon. You may want to put it in a waterproof bag—unless you are positive it won't rain.
6. Perform a Release Ritual: Write down the things that need letting go. Light the paper on fire and place it in a fireproof container. Watch the ash and smoke take your troubles away into the arms of the full moon.

Disseminating Moon

The disseminating moon phase is demonstrative and receptive. It is associated with transformation, communication, and the sharing of resources. It is the time in the lunar cycle to progress toward advancing your goals by adjusting any action you took during the full moon phase that didn't lead exactly to the intended outcome. The questions to ask yourself during the disseminating moon phase are: Did my goals contribute to the welfare of others? Did my idealism turn toward self-righteous indignation? During this lunar phase, you will see a clear picture of the lessons you've learned through your life experiences and self-awareness. Teach others what you have learned. Make an offering to the moon by gathering feathers, leaves, branches, shells, and place them on a stone altar under the Moon or a tree stump as an altar. If they are not available, create a sacred circle on the ground and place your offering in the middle. Express your gratitude to Mother Moon for her love and support.

Disseminating Moon

The disseminating moon connects to the first quarter phase of the lunar cycle and the awareness of the movement or position of your body. It represents the challenge of aligning your personal vision with the needs of the collective. Move your body through sport or dance to unblock and align your chakras. Share your knowledge and visit old friends. Demonstrate your appreciation to Mother Moon by giving back to your community. be grateful for everything you have, all the special intentions you worked for, and acknowledge the importance of being hopeful for the future.

Last Quarter Moon

The last quarter or third quarter moon phase is about spiritual healing and the advent of the time where you need to move forward, let go of past pain and feelings that caused you to hurt. The last quarter lunar phase is leading you toward redirection, accepting responsibility for your actions, transition-ning, and completion. It is a time to draw on your inner strength to acknowledge any mistakes made and reward yourself for your successes. During this lunar phase, it's a time to get creative and be willing to take some risks. You may need to change some aspects of the foundation you have already built. You do this by figuring out what is working for you and what isn't working for you. Then take corrective action or make that final push toward successful completion. Then it is time to ask yourself, "Now what?"

Last Quarter Moon

The last quarter moon phase connects to your senses, touch, smell, and taste. Using your senses will help you successfully complete the cycle's goals. If your senses or your energy feels blocked, you can release it with tactile activities, such as seeing a chiropractor or a massage therapist, and through using your sense of smell with aromatherapy. The last quarter lunar phase symbolizes the end of the Moon's journey. For us, it means the last stage when you complete your work or when your efforts seeded under the new moon blossom.

Balsamic Moon

The balsamic moon is the final phase of the waning half of the lunar cycle before the new beginnings and fresh starts come along with the energy of the new moon. It symbolizes recovery and healing, time to yield and repose. It is a time to avoid taking actions that hurt you and to be still and at peace. This lunar phase encompasses the 3 Rs:

1. Rest: Get a good night's sleep and frequent rest periods during the day.
2. Rejuvenate: Plan a feel good activity, such as a massage or spend some alone time at the beach. Practice self-love.
3. Release: Let go of things that are not serving you. Visualize these things, write them down and burn them under the moon. Declutter your home, car, and office. Rid yourself of anything weighing you down so you can create new space for the fresh beginnings and energy that come with the new moon.

Balsamic Moon

Special Moon Phases

When you take an interest in looking up at the night sky, chances are you will notice that the Moon never really looks the same as the night before. Even though a full moon means the face of the Moon is lit up completely by the Sun, not all full moons appear the same. Sometimes the Moon is glowing red, sometimes it looks huge. The Moon isn't actually changing size or color, it is where it is situated in relation to the Earth and Sun that affects its appearance to us. The following are some special moon phases, so you can set your magical intentions accordingly.

Blood Moon   Super Moon   Blue Moon   Harvest Moon

Blood Moon

Quite obviously, the reason why the blood moon is named so is that it glows red. A truly spectacular sight to see. I even set my alarm just in case I am sleeping to get up and spend some time with her. This special blood moon happens when there is a total lunar eclipse. The Earth is lined up between the Sun and the Moon, so the Moon is hidden from the sunlight. The only sunlight that reaches the surface of the Moon is from the outskirt of the Earth's atmosphere. The Earth's atmospheric air molecules scatter and block out the blue-colored light, leaving only the red reflection from the Sun, and the Moon glowing red. It is also called a blood moon when the smoke, haze, and dust in the sky make it appear reddish. Also, when the autumn leaves are turning red, the full moon is referred to as a blood moon.

During a blood moon, it is time to celebrate life, the blood running through your veins that is keeping you alive, and to make peace with your past. Use your spell crafting to increase your intuition and psychic abilities. The blood moon phase of the Moon is well suited for healing rituals and magic, specifically those pertaining to female issues, such as menstrual problems and reproductive health. Blood moon rituals invoking a deity or deities you feel closely connected to, or to perform other rituals designed to invoke the goddesses or gods of your tradition that are amplified during a blood moon.

Super Moon

A Super moon appears in the sky as a much larger-than-usual Moon. This is because it is closer to us. Astronomers refer to a super moon as a perigean full moon, which is a moon at its fullest and is at its closest orbital point around the Earth.

Super Moon

Supermoon Magic

1. Work with the element of water. Due to the exceptionally strong gravitational pull, the supermoon creates on the ocean tides, it is the perfect time to spellcraft with the element water.
    a. Springwater: Best for creativity, inspiration, and new beginnings spells.

    b. Rain Water: Best for garden magic, moon rituals, and house cleansing rituals.

    c. Ocean Water: Best for love spells, honoring or invoking sea deities, and power rituals.

2. Burn super moon incense anywhere in your home or on your altar.

    a. Combine equal parts dried lavender, cinnamon, and mugwort for the super moon. Burn it as a background to draw the super moon's energies or burn during a super moon ceremony.

3. Super Moon Cookie Recipe: Perfect for any witch, especially a kitchen witch. All you have to do is take your favorite cookie dough or cookie recipe and instead of making a batch of cookies, make one huge cookie. Just make sure it is thin enough not to be doughy in the middle. Offer to your family or your coven during the super moon.

4. Magnify the power of the super moon. Take a magnifying glass and charge your altar, objects, crystals, wands, you name it, and raise the power of the super moon by catching its light with your magnifying glass.

5. Perform a dedication or rededication. Ready to commit to a coven, deity, or a cause? Do so under the illumination of the super moon.

6. Drawing down the moon is an activity where you call a deity directly into your body. When conducted by a High Priestess or Priest, they are literally drawing the goddess into their body. Once the goddess is present, the Priestess or Priest is absent, and the goddess will speak directly through her daughter or son and interact with others at the ceremony. It is usually conducted at closed rituals with highly experienced members, as it is exhausting hard work, so if you are a newbie, give it some time.
7. Make super moon water. You can just place your water under the super moon overnight or you can use the following recipe:

Frank's Blessed by the Supermoon Water

a. You'll need:
   i. Super moon
   ii. Clear quartz or moonstone crystal
   iii. Lavender flower or drop of lavender essential oil
   iv. Cinnamon stick or pinch of cinnamon
   v. Glass container
   vi. Cauldron or pot
   vii. Strainer

    viii. Funnel
    ix. Floating white candle
- b. Directions
    i. Gather your ingredients
    ii. Boil the water and the herbs
    iii. Simmer for 30 minutes
    iv. Allow to cool and strain into your container(s)
    v. Place your containers where you can see the super moon's reflection onto it
    vi. Put your crystal in the water.
    vii. Light your white floating candle
    viii. Thank the super moon, meditate, and put the candle out
    ix. Remove the candle wax the next morning.
    x. Pour your super moon blessed water into a glass container or corked glass bottle.
    xi. Use for spellwork, charging items, drinking, etc.

Blue Moon

We have all heard the phrase "nce in a blue moon." That phrase was actually documented as early as the year 1528. When there are two full moons in a lunar cycle, the second one is called a blue moon. A blue moon is much more powerful than a full moon and promotes powerful and significant spells. A blue moon only happens every 2 anf a half years. Spells and magic that happen during the blue moon often have long-term consequences, so remember that and don't use a spell when you are not sure about the effects. Meditation during this moon phase, as is divination, because of your heightened power is very important.

As I just mentioned, a blue moon is given to the second full moon that happens in the same month, but it was first given to any extra full moon that occurred in a season. Modern-day Wicca associates the blue moon with the growth of knowledge and wisdom. Pagan folklore provided names for moon phases to help people get ready for crop rotations and varying types of weather. The Moon has usually been connected to the mysteries, divine aspects, and intuition of the sacred feminine. In the Wiccan religion, it is sometimes associated with elderly women, and it is referred to as the grandmother aspect of the Triple Goddess. One thing is for sure, you can expect a boost in your magical workings during a blue moon. It is the perfect time for communicating with the spirit world and developing your psychic abilities. The blue moon inspires you to embrace your uniqueness and make any necessary tweaking to support your personal intentions.

Magical Practices for the Blue Moon

1. Take a spiritual blue moon cleansing bath using peppermint and chamomile. You can use essential oils, but for an extra special time use actual peppermint leaves and chamomile flowers.
2. Make a list of things weighing you down and that are no longer doing you any good and then burn it.
3. Meditated under the blue moon by connecting with its divine energy.
4. Write your intentions on a piece of paper and ask the blue moon out loud to manifest your desires.

5. Put on a blindfold, crank up the music, and dance.
6. Frank's Blue Moon Ritual
   a. What you'll need
      i. A candle
      ii. Flowers, according to the season.
      iii. A printed out image of the Empress tarot card.
      iv. Sea salt
      v. Sage Incense, or you can smudge with a sage bundle.
   b. Directions: Place all of your ingredients on your altar and chant these words out loud:

   Empress of beauty, balance, and grace
   Release my baggage, so I can pick up my pace
   Drive them down deep into precious Mother Earth
   So the next moon cycle, I can experience rebirth
   So mote it be.

Dark Moon

The dark moon is actually a waning crescent moon that happens just before the new moon lunar phase. It is called dark because it doesn't reflect much light and is barely visible. Hence it is a time when many people will be feeling dark as well. It represents the dark aspects of the moon goddess pertaining to death and destructive magic. The dark moon is associated with stillness, introspection, soul searching, meditation, and dark magic. During the dark moon, go to bed early and get up late—radical rest is necessary. Spend some time consulting your runes, tarot, or oracle cards and tune into your intuition.

Dark Moon

Witchcraft you can do: hexes, curses, banishing, divorce, separation, and protection spells. This is a good time to meditate and perform divination rituals to get a glimpse into the future and see what awaits you. Cancel any plans you may have and spend time doing shadow work.

Shadow Work

1. Practice mindfulness
2. Invoke Hecate and ask her to please cast light on the shadow side of the challenges you are facing and to guide you through the struggles.
3. Create an altar especially for doing shadow work, a sacred space where you can explore the shadows.
4. Work with crystals that correspond with the dark moon, such as black obsidian, snowflake obsidian, rose quartz, and blue kyanite.
5. Paint, draw, journal, or write to tap into your shadow side. If you're feeling too positive, let yourself welcome those shadows that are within. It is a time for self-reflection. Once you become familiar with your shadows, you can communicate to the Universe or your deities what you want to work on.

Lunar Eclipse

Since we know that the moon doesn't emit any of its own light, what we do see is the Sun's reflection off the moon's surface. When a lunar eclipse happens, the shadow of the Earth is blocking the Sun's rays, causing the Moon to darken temporarily. The good news is that everyone can see it, unlike a solar eclipse, which can only be seen by some.

Some of today's witchcraft traditions feel that a lunar eclipse amplifies the power of your intentions, kind of like a cosmic bonus round. However, lately, there has been some discussion that practicing magic during the lunar eclipse is dangerous if you're a newbie witch. This is positively untrue. If you think that somehow your psyche can be damaged by the strength of lunar eclipse magic, please reconsider practicing magic at all. That type of thinking can self-sabotage your spell casting and ritual workings. I would recommend practicing your grounding techniques to safeguard against self-sabotage. Actually, lunar eclipse magic does wonders for spiritual development and personal growth rituals.

The lunar eclipse is moon phase brimming with magic power. It happens once every year, and its magical powers are associated with change and symbolize major shifts in your life.

Lunar eclipse moon magic can include but is not limited to the following:

- Healing rituals or magic
- Drawing down the moon
- Drawing money
- Healing relationships
- Protection spells
- Spells to increase your psychic abilities
- Spells to raise your intuitive awareness
- Divination
- Asking Mother Moon for wisdom.
- Spells to boost your magical skill set.
- Rituals to honor lunar goddesses and gods.

CHAPTER 2:
MOON SPELLCASTING: COMMON TOOLS AND PREPARATION

The only real required tool or ingredient for all magic is your intention. Any ingredient or object can become energetically and magically charged, so you don't have to buy the most expensive healing crystals or a $500 crystal ball. Cayenne pepper, cinnamon, sugar, and sage are powerful ingredients that can be used in a variety of infusions, oils, and potions. You can make just about any candle into a magically charged device. It is totally up to you, as long as you are confident in what it means to set your intention, cleanse your items, and make magic, you are good to go. After all, a cooking pot can become your cauldron, and a stick from the yard your wand. The magic is inside you.

Moon Altars

Similar to setting up any sacred altar, a moon altar is a magical place for you to harness and hone the various energies of the lunar cycle. A sacred moon altar is a place that you can focus, direct, and deliver your energy through your magical practice of witchcraft. You can perform meditations, rituals, and spells at your moon altar, or simply use it as a place of lunar worship. There is really no wrong way to set up your moon altar. It can be outside or inside, simple or elaborate, and anything in between. There are specific magical tools you can place on your altar that will definitely add focus and power to your moon magic, so get as innovative and creative as you want when setting up your moon altar, as long as it feels special, powerful, and sacred to you.

Types of Moon Altars

1. *Traveling Moon Altars*: You can carry your witchcraft tools with you anywhere you go. Simply take a drawstring bag and put some magical essence in it, such as a cinnamon stick or a few leaves from my favorite herb plant. Make sure to use travel-friendly tools in your bag, such as your runes, small gems, birthday candles, tarot cards, coins, colored ribbon. All of these tools are perfect for carrying with you to set up an altar somewhere in a natural setting under the moon.
2. *Stationary Moon Altar*: This is your usual altar set up in your home or office, only you are using magical tools specific for lunar rituals. I have a permanent altar set up in my dining room, near the patio, just to pay respect to every phase of the moon. The ideal aspect of a stationary altar is that you can deck them out with all different types of tools and trinkets without having to worry about damaging or losing any of your devices while traveling.

3. *Mental Altars*: Slightly less conventional, a mental altar may appeal to witches who are very good at and love visualizing. In your mind's eye, you can imagine your moon altar by picturing your sacred space, visualizing your tools, and placing it anywhere in the world you can imagine. A mental altar is a good form of lunar meditation, which goes perfectly with a lunar bath—bathing in the moonlight—or for divination rituals under the moon.

Altar Accessories

Along with candle holders for rituals to light candles, incense burners for spells require burning incense, crystals, and vases for flowers there are meanings behind each accessory.

Wands: direct energy, bless something, and consecrate sacred spaces or magical items

Frank's Wand

According to Gardnerian Wicca, the wand corresponds with the elements Air and Fire. I have a special wand for moon magic. It is oak and has a small, clear quartz on one tip that reminds me of the moon, and when I hold it up to certain moons, I can see its reflection glowing on the tip of the crystal. In Gerald Gardner's *Book of Shadows* (1950), he said his wand was "used to summon certain spirits." The same goes with my wand. I use it to summon the elements and the Moon. The element fire represents energy and power; hence the Wiccan wand is a magical tool used for directing your will and energy. Like the Moon, the witch's wand is strongly associated with magical transformation. Traditionally magic wands are used for many purposes in Wiccan rituals, and most are related to the direction or channeling of power and energy. Keep your wand on your moon altar and use it to cast your circle for your lunar rituals and to create your invisible, protective barrier around you when you practice your magic. Harness the vibrational energy of Mother Moon to direct its healing powers and to cast your spells.

Grimoire or Book of Shadows, you can use a notebook to document your lunar magical practices and spell work.

A Witch's Grimoire on Lunar Spells

Despite popular belief and things you see in the movies, there is not no single Wiccan Book of Shadows. Keeping a lunar grimoire is a perfect place to keep your moon spells, lunar correspondences and charts, invocations, ritual practices, a list of lunar magic rules, your favorite legends and myths, various pantheons, and anything else that can help you power up for the magic that comes with each phase of the Moon. Sometimes, a Lunar Book of Shadow's information can be passed along from one coven or Wiccan to another. Your lunar grimoire should be very personal to you. Once you have one, if you don't already have one, place it on your altar and perform this blessing ritual before and after your lunar spells:

In the Moon's magic realm, this book shall reside.

Only the Moon and the chosen can see what's inside.
Mother Moon protects it and shelters it from harm.
From moon phase to moon phase, it's blessed with her charm.
This grimoire is mine and contains no fears
My spells and my magic the moon goddess hears.
So mote it be

Crystals for Moon Magic

Crystals Corresponding with the Moon

There are various ways to use crystals in your moon magic and lunar rituals. Place a charged crystal corresponding with your intention in the center of your altar. I usually write my intention on a piece of paper and place it under the stone. In my humble opinion, I think that when you're working with different lunar phases, it is not so much about the particular crystal you pick to work with, because there are quite a few, but it is more about the intention you set for working with that specific lunar phase. In general, there are several gemstones that have vibrational frequencies that correspond with the moon, and it doesn't matter which lunar phase is occurring at that particular moment. The following are the crystals I recommend because their energies are specific to particular phases of the moon, but by no means are these the only crystals that work magic with the moon:

- *Selenite* is named after Selene, the Greek moon goddess. You can use it for amplifying moonlight, and moon energy, protection, and uplifting your mood. It is also great for charging and cleansing the other stones and tools you are working with.
- *Moonstone* is as ancient as the moon itself. When used for lunar magic, it can be used to guide and heal your inner journey, nourish your spirituality, and amp up your passion. With a waxing and waning moon, it has an esoteric, sensual feel as it evokes the peacefulness and tranquility of the moon. It releases a glowing surge of energy that can revitalize the body and mind and rinse away

negativity. Moonstone crystals are enveloped by powerful rays of purple, blue, and gold and it is perpetually embraced by a glowing white energy making it a protective stone.

- *Labradorite* is a favorite crystal for any season or occasion, but it really shines when it comes to moon magic. It represents awareness, new beginnings, psychic powers, motivation for going after your heart's desires, and visioning. This gem, when utilized for a new moon ritual, embodies possibilities and potential for your future, but also enhances your visions, and fires up your inner spirit like the brilliant flashes of fiery color that sparkles from the darkness of the stone. It activates your senses and unblocks the third eye chakra. Place it on your moon altar and let the stone guide your way through any struggles or challenges pointed in your direction.
- *Opal* is Australia's national gemstone and has been used in witchcraft since ancient times where it was known as a symbol of faithfulness and confidence. Opal was believed to have descended from the heavens onto Arabia as bolts of lightning. It was referred to as the *eye stone* during the middle ages, where it was used in magic to remedy

poor eyesight. Use opal in your full moon rituals to summon the powers of the moon goddess. They can also be used to magically draw money from the moon.

- *Clear Quartz* is used in moon magic for its pure healing energy that supports the spirit, as well as the mind and body. Under a new moon, it draws away any discomfort or pain, and washes away negativity. It's a powerful amplifier and strongly enhances the moon's energies to their fullest potential.

Athames and other blades indicate directions and direct energies. Bladed tools represent masculine energy and the element air.

Lunar Altar with Athame

Athames are used in many pagan and Wiccan rituals as tools for circle casting and directing energy. It is a double-edged dagger that you can buy or have made by hand. The anthem is associated with air and fire, depending on your tradition. Pre-Wiccan traditions, such as the Hermetic Order of the Golden Dawn link it with the element air because its sharpness directs energy by moving it in the air, and sharpness is also connected to high intellect — as in sharp-minded. Because the dagger is forged in fire, many pagans believe it is connected to the element fire. For eclectic witches, you can just choose whichever makes sense to your intuition.

Chalice or goblet: a symbol of the goddess and her womb, it also symbolizes the element water.

Chalice preparing Moon Bless Water

The chalice, or goblet, is found in many pagan and Wiccan goddess-oriented traditions. Along with the cauldron, the chalice represents the womb and is considered feminine as a vessel in which life begins. The chalice corresponds with the element water and is perfect for preparing moon-blessed water recipes, such as the one in chapter one. I have a pewter chalice, but many of my friends have silver, ceramic, or wooden ones. I recommend keeping one on your lunar altar specifically for moon-based magic. If you are having a moon party, you can pass the chalice around and each participant can sip from the moon-blessed water. It will empower and bless anyone who drinks from it. It is a great moon-bonding activity where words like "may you never feel tired or thirsty" are spoken within a sacred circle under the Moon. Just make sure if you are drinking from your chalice that it is not made of any material containing lead.

Cauldrons are an essential tool for witchcraft and spell-making. It can be used to burn incense and herbs, brew potions, and perform water scrying to enhance vision.

Cauldron

Cauldrons are large pots, usually made of metal with a handle and a lid used to brew over an open fire. Dating back at least to the Bronze Age, the word *cauldron* is derived from old Germanic and Norse words meaning "hot place" (OtherWorldly.com, 2019). Back in time, there was no electricity, so the cauldron came as a great blessing for cooking and became associated with feminine magic or women's magic, and later witch's magic.

Magical Uses for Witch's Cauldron

- Cook moon food. There's nothing like making a cheese fondue to celebrate the moon being made of cheese. Sometimes, these somewhat silly stories that have been passed down through the generations are taken on as terms of endearment. It's a great way to celebrate a full moon with a belly full of cheese, especially if you have a Wiccan or pagan family. Children love dancing around a bonfire and dipping apples into the melted cheese in honor of a moon ritual.

- Brew concoctions and herbal remedies in honor of the moon gods or goddesses—or for healing purposes. Craft your concoctions and herbal remedies using healing, vibrational, and magical ingredients for your intended purpose. I create mine for clearing and healing, and you can too. Clear away things that aren't serving you. Making a full moon elixir is great for any lunar ritual and will intensify the magic even after the moon has set. You can make potions with your favorite herbs and some olive oil or coconut oil for topical use, or an elixir with basil, mint, cinnamon, and spring water. Just concoct it under the moon and leave in the moonlight for at least one night.
- Burn Incense
- Burn papers with written petitions on them.
- Burn offerings, such as plant matter.
- A safe place to leave a lit candle overnight.
- You can scrape the bottom and use the scraps to make black witch's salt.

- Use it as a symbol on your altar for the moon goddess or for the elements during your lunar ritual.
- Hold your moon collection aromatic potpourri.

Moon Magic With Herbs, Flowers, and Plants

Altar Herbs

If you use plants, flowers, or herbs in your lunar rituals, you can arrange them in the shape of the moon phase under which you are crafting. I love to arrange a circle of dandelions on my altar when there is a full moon and jasmine in the shape of a crescent waxing or waning moon! Fresh herbs, plants, and flowers really make an incredible difference in the way I feel when I am performing a lunar ritual.

Another magical boost you can do with herbs, plants, and flowers is to represent the phase of the moon with the phase of the flower. Seeds and buds represent a new moon. Flowers just starting to bud for a waxing moon, and flowers in full bloom for a full moon. I take the petals of the flowers after they fall off or they're wilting and spread them around my moon altar to symbolize a waning moon.

Placing herbs, plants, and flowers on your moon altar symbolize Mother Earth and each of them has their own magical properties. In order for your lunar rituals to be successful, it's a good idea to pick up the herbs, plants, or flowers that match the moon's phase and your personal intentions. For instance, Sage and lavender are good for a lunar cleansing ritual, they both blow away negativity and help to purify limiting thoughts. For protection from Mother Moon, practice your lunar magic with mint and garlic. If you are asking Mother Moon for love, use coriander and cinnamon. If you are working on a project place violet on your altar as it corresponds with creativity. Ginger and dill on your moon altar make for successful business ventures, and to sharpen up your intuition—and for better sleep—adorn your moon altar with chamomile.

Boline: for cutting herbs.

Boline

While there is no fast or hard rule as to what tool to use when cutting your herbs, Wicca tradition recommends using a boline as your magical cutting tool, for harvesting your herbs for lunar rituals. The best time to harvest them for your lunar altar is early in the day before the sun has a chance to dry them out. This way the herbs will keep their aroma and essential oils, which is an important instrument for moon magic. The oils are what maintains the fragrance. Cut and collect only the herbs you need that correspond with your intention for your lunar witchcraft. Certain herbs such as rosemary are best to snip off as an entire stem, but others, like basil, you can run your fingers down the stem and collect the leaves. Using your boline to manicure your plants will boost their magic. If you take a look at the image of a boline above, you will notice it is shaped like a crescent moon. If you are going to use your boline for flowers, such as lilacs or chamomile, wait until they are in full bloom to cut them. If you are performing a new moon ritual and using the seeds, make sure they are completely developed. I take a paper bag and place it over the head of my plants, such as on the dill plant, and shake it. The dry seeds easily come loose into the paper bag.

Compasses: helps you move in the right direction, harness the right energies, and help you to align yourself properly.

Witch's Compass

The magical circle is a part of the narrative and heritage of witchcraft. Historically, there are hundreds of examples of witches gathering in a circle to feast, work magic, dance, and yes, worship the

Moon. The same applies to today's magical practices. Within the realm of traditional Wicca lies the concept of the witch's compass. It is a way to mark out or delineate the sacred working ground and separate it from unsacred space. I have heard Wiccans describe the compass as being a space between the Earth and the spirit world, for within the circle, witches can invoke many spirits, commune with divinity, and summon magical forces.

In some Wiccan traditions, the compass is made up of three rings surrounding a fixed center point. Each of the rings symbolizes a different stage in the life cycle. Therefore, they are designed as working from the outside moving inwards toward the center point as a symbolic pathway through the stages of life and into the spirit realm. You can make your own rings. The first is made of salt, symbolizing life. The second is made of wood ash symbolizing death and rebirth. The third ring is made of wine, salt, and water and represents the waterway we use to crossover to the spiritual realm.

Candlelight Represents Moonlight

Lunar Altar Candles

Since candlelight represents moonlight, you can use any kind of candle as a magical tool. I like to use white tea lights because they remind me of little moons. They make black ones, too for when there is a new moon. You can also make your own moon candles for divination or spells. Burning your intentions with your moon candle is a fantastic magical activity. Candle gazing and moon gazing at the same time is an incredibly powerful meditation. For a full moon and a waxing moon, light a candle, and leave it unlit during a new moon or a waning moon.

If you are using a new candle, place it on your moon altar and smudge it or light some incense around it to energetically cleanse it. This also creates a wonderful aroma for your moon ritual to come. Next, you'll want to infuse your intention into your candle for the upcoming lunar phase. What are your dreams and hopes for the next couple of weeks? How can you navigate this lunar cycle with authenticity and strength? Journal your thoughts on these types of questions. That's right, get writing! Try to come up with a single word that encompasses what you want to manifest with your lunar intention. Then, scribe your word, your initials, and a symbol onto your candle, or draw a tiny moon in the phase that you are going to be casting your spells. Candles summon deities, work your manifestations, represent the element fire in spells and rituals, and symbolize gods and goddesses in Wicca. Anoint your candle with olive oil or essential oils.

Burin: used to carve symbols into candles, wood, and other magical objects.

Burin

A burin is a sharp tool with a pointed end used for ceremonial magic and witchcraft for marking, carving, and scribing magical items such as your candles. Wiccan traditions engrave symbols and signs into their wooden wands, and the candles they used for lunar worship. Similar to the white-handled knife used by covens for many rituals, the burin can be used as a personal tool at home by witches, whereas the white-handled knife can only be used inside of a sacred circle during a ritual.

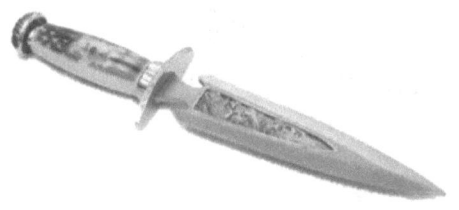

Wiccan White-Handled Knife

Broom or Besom: for cleaning dirt, negative energies, and removing bad influences before lunar magic and spell work.

Besom

An essential tool for your lunar rituals is the witch's besom or broom. We've all grown up with Halloween pictures of the witch flying on her broom across the front of the Moon, which is actually documented in art from the early fifteenth century (Gannon, 2013). The hallowed instruments of magic have been used since ancient times to sweep out negativity while sweeping in happiness and prosperity. Wiccans consider their besoms to be so powerful that filling it with intention makes it come true.

Bells and Rattles: used to summon spirits, get rid of dark energies. and evil presence. Rattles and singing bowls bring peace and harmony to a sacred space or cleanse a magical ritual.

Witch's Bells and Rattle

In paganism and Wicca, handbells have historically been used for ritual. The sound of vibrations given off by the ringing of bells has been believed to ward off evil spirits, and possess spiritual or magical powers for centuries. The sounds of the witch's bells represent creative power and are kindred with the divine. Keep them on your altar for use during lunar rituals to bring harmony and boost your powers. Dance with your bells under the moon to invoke the moon gods and goddesses. The sound of a rattle also causes vibrations that are a great source of power for communing with the moon goddess. In some Wiccan covens, a bell tolls 40 times to summon the dead the members one wishes to honor. You can use your anthem or any of your other magical tools to sound your bells and rattles.

Clothes: for lunar rituals. It can be a cloak, robe, or mask that will help you achieve the right mindset to perform the magic.

Ritual Robe

Something can be said for wearing lunar ritual robes or cloaks, as they have been worn by pagans and Wiccans for centuries as a way of separating themselves from an ordinary day and enhancing their sense of mystery and magic. Donning a cloak is as much a part of the spiritual and mental preparation for lunar ritual as it is to dress your lunar altar. Some witches prefer ritual robes for their moon magic practices. It is a personal choice, but many witches I know who practice Wiccan tradition, do not wear anything underneath. But a cloak usually only fastens at the neck, so you might not want to be naked. As always, do what makes you feel most comfortable.

Robes can be handmade or purchased. There are loads of patterns online that are simple to assemble if you're like me and not a very experienced sewer. You can wear any color cloak to match your lunar phase worship or your intuition. Both white and blue correspond with the Moon. But I have seen pink cloaks and bright yellow ones too. Make one hundred percent sure that you have non-flammable clothing on for any ritual, as candles and bonfires can lead to accidental problems, especially when there is a breeze. Most have hoods and sleeves, but if you live in a hot climate you can find them without.

Spears: popular witchcraft tools for Wiccans that represent the Horned God in rituals.

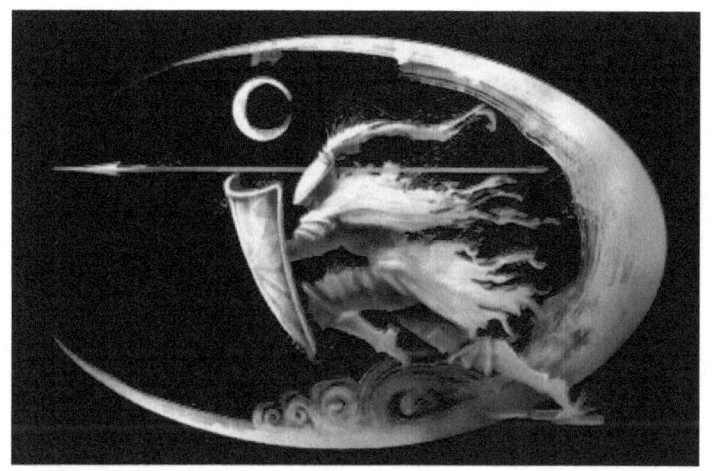

Witch's Spear

The spear is documented all the way back to 400,000 BC (Ingenito, 2021). It was used as a hunting tool and a weapon. You can make a symbolic small spear to place on your lunar altar to honor the Horned God and to focus your intention upon during a crescent moon ritual. Wiccan symbols such as a spear represent the Horned God and therefore correspond with a crescent moon phase. Your life experiences as a pagan or a Witch, your knowledge, and your present understanding of symbolic tools play a role in how you identify with each magical item on your lunar altar.

Offering Bowls: used for making offerings to the gods and goddesses.

Offering Bowl on Lunar Altar

For my lunar offerings, I collect stones, feathers, fallen leaves, a palm frond or two, sometimes on a new moon an egg, that I bury after the ritual. I do this for the days preceding the ritual and place it on my lunar altar. I surround my bowl with flower petals, candles, and crystals. I also put a nice crystal cup for my moon-blessed water to charge. All of the items will be charged during any lunar phase ritual. I know some witches who love to fill their offering bowls with delightful delectables, such as chocolate truffles, and other guilty pleasures made of cacao, in honor of the moon. Cacao translates to "the food of the gods and goddesses" in the ancient Aztec language.

Pen and Paper: an essential item to have on your lunar altar to pen down the intentions, dreams, desires, and emotions you want to get rid of, along with many other aspects of your magical desires.

Pen and Paper

Penning down your thoughts on a piece of paper is in itself a magical ritual. Learning how to draw sigils and symbols is a fascinating and spiritual process as well as an educational one. Drawing the phase of the moon you are about to perform in color for your ritual is part of focusing on the intention of your lunar magic. Drawing a hill with the moon setting upon it, or the moon shining through some tree branches, inspires your moon-given creativity and is enacting your artistic expression at the same time. It honors Mother Moon. Writing down your intention and its desired outcome is one of the best ways to clearly and specifically communicate what you want out of your lunar magic. It is like writing a note for Mother Moon to read herself. Another reason writing down your intention is a good idea is because by doing so you avoid an accidental manifestation of something you didn't want. For instance, if you are performing a money drawing lunar spell, you want to specifically ask for a large amount of money or you may end up winning a hundred dollar lottery ticket that will not help you out of a financial bind as I did.

Formula for Writing Out Intention:

In the present tense, using the word *I*, write your specific desire + the time frame you want it to manifest. This is your intention.

For instance: "I drive a blue Ford Mustang to work every day" is more powerful than "I need a new car."

Intention Setting Lunar Ritual

1. Perform this ritual under the Moon on a blanket or sitting on the Earth, where you won't be disturbed.
2. Light three white candles and place them safely around you in a circle.

3. Make a ceremonial tea with a few drops of almond extract and some fresh mint, hopefully from your lunar garden.
4. Journal by penning down what your life looks like at the present moment. What type of relationship you are in, how you spend your leisure time, in general how you are feeling.
5. Next, moon-gaze, focusing on how you want your life to be after you have manifested your intention.
6. Write down your intention following the formula above, filling in the gaps of what you wrote in what your life looks like now and what you wrote for how you want it to be after your manifested desire.

Pentacles and Pentagrams: represent the elements at each of its points, and are used for blessing items and tools, and charging objects, like crystals and chalices. Deeply ingrained in history, the pentagram is documented in artifacts from as far back as 3000 BC and was used in religious rituals by the ancient Greeks, and the ancient Babylonians. It is also documented in early Christian works for over five centuries as a symbol of the five wounds of Jesus Christ (Dual Crossroads.com., 2021).

Pentagram at Lunar Ritual

In Wiccan and pagan traditions, the pentagram symbol is not a representation of good versus evil. It is a symbol of the elements water, fire, earth, air, and spirit—with one point representing each element. The circle is symbolic of the Universe that holds and connects them all. The pentacle is a symbol of faith. One common misconception about the pentagram in Wicca is the direction in which it points. Pointing down does not mean toward the devil, and it should not be associated with Satanism. This misconception came about in 1966 due to the established Church of Satan, which endorsed the inverted pentagram encircling a goat's head as its symbol (Criger, 2021). In Wicca, the top point of the pentagram symbolizes the element air and corresponds with the spirit ascending above.

Lunar Calendars: detail the phases of the moon, help you prepare the spells rituals so that each spell will be cast at the right time in order for you to get the desired results.

Lunar Phase Calendar

As the Moon orbits the Earth—and the Earth orbits the Sun—over the course of the month we experience each of the Moon's phases. As the Moon takes its sweet time radiating, renewing, resetting, retreating, and resting every 29 days, so do we. We traverse different mindsets, ways of acting, and emotional experiences. We move or orbit around those experiences the same way the Moon moves or orbits the Earth. The more aligned we are with those phases and how they attune with us, the better able we are at harnessing moon magic. If you take into consideration each of the moon's phases and their particular energies, you have an opportunity to tailor your magical practices and witchcraft for each new phase of the moon. Keeping notes and keeping your eye on your lunar calendar is the best way to stay mindful of each lunar event. I hang mine just above my lunar altar.

Preparing for Moon Spells

Preparing for lunar rituals around the Moon's energy has been a tradition across cultures of the world since ancient times. All around the Earth, all people are under the same moon, illuminating our evening skies to eventually become swallowed in darkness, only to miraculously start to grow again. Each lunar phase describes a different quality or energy, either receding or building, and specific rituals can be enacted to call upon those energies around each phase. Prepare yourself spiritually and mentally for your lunar spell castings, so you can achieve your desired outcome.

Whether you belong to a coven or you are a solitary witch, you can use your lunar calendar to pinpoint the moment the moon is new or full, so you can be as exact as you want to be for your ritual. The Moon represents your inner-being, and some of these traits you may keep safely hidden away from the rough exterior of the outside world. Vulnerability is an attribute associated with the Mother Moon or the moon priestesses. The Moon's element is water, corresponding to your emotional energies swelling and then receding like the tides. Deep feelings and sometimes sadness are expressed elementally in your emotions, and inturn, are welcomed in by the moon's circle.

Preparations

- Cleanse sacred spaces by smudging and lighting incense on your altar
- Choose the right time
- Find the right location
- Review the spell
- Prepare the tools
- Correct your state of mind. Focus your mind on the loyal companionship of the Moon. It

never leaves you. It is always watching over you, steadfast, knowing your darkest moments, as well as your light. It changes just as you do, with every day being a different version of itself. Just like you, sometimes it is strong and bright; and sometimes just like you, it is waning and weak. The Moon reflects humanity, and all that it means to be human. What it means to feel alone and unsure, and cratered with imperfections.

Ritual Practices for Each Moon Phases

- New Moon - Set and reset intentions
- Waxing Crescent - Practice self-love and nurture your new ideas.
- First Quarter - Start action
- Waxing Gibbous - Refine and formulate your plans
- Full Moon - Illuminate and manifest your intentions
- Waning Gibbous - Reap the rewards of your lunar magic and express your gratitude to god and goddess.

- Last Quarter - Let go of things no longer serving you and release energy.
- Waning Crescent - Celebrate completing your cycle and get some much needed rest.

CHAPTER 3:
NEW MOON SPELLS

Did you know that you can use the lunar phases to manifest love, draw money, find a new job, and many other manifestations that come true because of new moon magic. Asking the Mother Moon to help you to start a new chapter in your life is best conducted during a new moon. It is the phase where rituals will help you to step into who you really are on a much deeper level. Understanding this phase of the Moon can provide you with success in your spell work, good fortune, and guidance from the goddess herself. It brings harmony, and makes you feel happier and energetic. The new moon phase is ideal for exacting, planning, and launching a business, it's great for money spells that will increase cash flow. Love spells are also a common practice during this lunar phase. Banishing spells, divination spells, and magic for fresh starts and new opportunities are all part of new moon rituals. Self-improvement spells—and curses—help you set goals during this stage of the Moon for the next upcoming cycle.

New Moon Spells, Rituals, and Ceremonies

Start with decluttering to prepare for the ritual: light a candle, burn sage, turn on relaxing music, keep pen and sacred paper you to write, connect with divine energy source you relate with or other deities that represent the moon. When everything is set, sit down and relax. Write down the details you want for the future and explore your life. Finally, after declaring your wishes, sit quietly and meditate.

Attracting a Lover Spell

This may seem like a very simple spell, but it is very useful and can be used for a variety of reasons that relate to attraction. Its intention is to attract your love interest to you; not only does it conjure up a lover, but it will bring you exactly what you ask for in a lover.

What You'll Need:

- New moon
- 4 red candles
- Pen and Paper
- 30 minutes of uninterrupted time
- Cinnamon essential oil

Directions:

1. Inscribe each red candle with a word, sigil, or symbol that represents your intentions.
2. Anoint your candles with cinnamon essential oil.
3. Set the marked candles in your sacred space side by side.
4. Write down your intention on a piece of paper. Be clear, concise, and focused.
5. Smudge your sacred space, and place your penned intention in between your arranged red candles.

6. Light all four candles, allowing the flame to settle into a balanced rhythm before carefully waving your intention over the flames of each red candle, consider using a pair of tongs for safety.
7. Let the fire completely burn your intentions, transmitting them to the lunar plane.
8. Be sure to practice caution when doing this, Use tongs or metal chopsticks to hold the paper and have a flameproof container to catch the ashes.
9. Take the ashes and throw them to the Moon while invoking the elements wind and fire to deliver your intention to the Mother Moon.
10. Place your candles in your cauldron and allow them to burn completely. Snuff them out if you do not have a fireproof container, but remember to use a cleansed tool to do so.

New Romance Spell

It's a quick and easy new romance love spell that dates back centuries to when witches infused honey into love potions under a new moon. Spell casters use honey to bring a couple closer to each other with its natural sweetness. One can use it on crushes, exes, and disgruntled romantic partners.

Moreover, consider the natural ingredient honey's stickiness to play a major role in gluing together a new romance

What You'll Need:

- A new moon
- A jar of honey
- A pen and paper

Directions:

1. Write your new lover's name three times on a piece of paper.
2. Rotate the paper 180 degrees, like the Moon rotates on its axis.
3. Write your name three times, overlapping the name of your new lover.
4. Focus on your intention on the new romance spell.
5. Write how you want your new romance to play out, in first person, present tense, and on the same paper as you and your new lover's names. Draw a circle around the two names representing the moon without lifting your pen.
6. Fold the paper gently and put it inside our honey jar.
7. Make sure to touch the honey with your fingers when you put the paper inside.

8. Chant this new romance incantation in a clear and loud voice:

   My new honey is so sweet,
   (new lover's name) is sweet love to me.
   So mote it be

9. Lick the honey off your fingers and then seal the jar with a lid or wax.
10. Rotate the jar in a circular motion symbolizing the moon before placing it on your lunar altar.
11. Thank the Mother Moon.

Facilitating Love Spell

This spell is best cast when the new moon is at its peak. However, if you can make it on that particular day, you can perform it one day before and one day after the new moon's maximum peak. To profoundly connect with this lunar phase, do this spell at night.

What You'll Need:

- New moon
- Red pen and paper
- Picture of your love interest
- One glass jar
- Petals of six dried roses
- Red piece of thread

- Three red candles

Directions:

1. Meditate and free yourself from all negativity and tension. Take your time.
2. Take a cleansing bath before you conduct this ritual.
3. Set up an outside moon altar and put your ingredients on it.
4. Smudge your altar and items.
5. Write your name and the name of the person with whom you are casting a facilitating love spell side by side.
6. Draw a red circle around both names.
7. Write on the back:

   With these names and these petals,
   this new love will settle, in both of our hearts,
   we will never part.
   So mote it be.

8. Roll the paper into a tube and tie the red string around it and then into a bow.
9. Place your scroll into the jar.
10. Make a triangle out of the red candles around the jar and light them.
11. Meditate on your love for 15 minutes
12. Snuff out the candles
13. Set the jar under the moon overnight.
14. In the morning, relight the candles.

15. Remove the scroll and use tongs to burn it.
16. Let the smoke and the ash take to the breeze.
17. Thank the Mother Moon for this new beginning.

Fertility Spell

What You'll Need:
- New Moon
- One brown egg
- Blue and pink pen and paper
- Angelica essential oil
- Cinnamon essential oil
- Mint leaves (a handful)
- Blue candle and pink candle

Directions:

1. Make a nest out of your mint leaves on your lunar altar for the egg.
2. Draw an interlocking male and female symbol on a piece of paper and place it on your mint nest.
3. Massage essential oils into your egg.
4. Place your egg into its nest
5. Light a candle on each side of the nest.

   I ask of you this night, oh special new moon
   To enter fertility into the womb

With passion and loyalty the new moon's stealth
To bring forth a baby in perfect health
So mote it be

6. Cook the egg the next day and eat it.

Authenticity Spell

Resetting boundaries, pronouncing your freedom, setting your intentions, and releasing your most authentic self for the month ahead is exactly what is asked of the new moon each month.

What You'll Need:

- New moon
- Pen and paper
- White candle

Directions:

1. Create a new moon mantra and keep it simple. Here are some examples:
    a. *I am a visionary who sees wonderful things coming my way.*
    b. *I am intuitive*
    c. *I am filled with brilliant authentic expressions.*
    d. *I live a prosperous life: rich with compassion, friends, money, and love*
    e. *I am the light of my soul.*
    f. *I am infinitely creative*

2. Write it on the paper.
3. Place the paper on your lunar altar
4. Light the white candle for five minutes each day for until the next lunar cycle according to your lunar calendar. It will keep your mantra alive.
5. Speak your mantra every evening under the new moon until the next moon phase.
6. Concentrate on asking Mother Moon to help you to live your most authentic self.

Job Hunting Spell

Hunting for a new job is much easier if you know how to align your intention and your energy with the vibrational energies of the new moon. Before you start this spell, spend a few moments determining the exact nature of the type of new job you want and the specific outcome you desire. Ask yourself, what are the benefits and salary you desire, what type of company you want to work for, and any other job concerns like the hours you prefer to work.

What You'll Need:

- New moon
- Pen
- Index card

- A green candle
- Honeysuckle essential oil
- Honeysuckle incense

Directions:

1. Light your incense and place it on your lunar altar. I have a small Aladdin's Lamp incense burner.
2. Write down on the index card the characterristics of the new job you want to attract.
3. Anoint the green candle with the honeysuckle essential oil, starting at the base and working up to the top using a clockwise motion.
4. Dab yourself in the center of your forehead, at the center of your heart, and on both temples with the oil.
5. In the evening under the new moon, hold the green candle with both hands, and visualize your intention and energy filling the candle. Focus on the pulsing and glowing acting like your beacon to the moon.
6. Place your candle on your lunar altar and light it.
7. Place the index card between your two hands and visualize already having your dream job. Picture yourself feeling excited,

blessed, eager, motivated, and elated just as you will when you get the job. Speak aloud:

Mother Moon, call forth the right job for me,
I am excited to become a new worker bee.
Using my talents, my strengths, and my gifts
Good money, good hours, no longer a myth.
So mote it be

New Moon Divination Spell

What You'll Need:

- New moon
- Candle holder
- White candle
- One deck of oracle cards of your choosing

Note: In case you are unfamiliar with the difference between an oracle deck and a tarot deck, let me give a quick explanation. Like a deck of tarot, oracle decks are illustrated beautifully, with many different themes—lunar included. Both are created to be able to pull a certain sense or intuition from the deck to aid you in answering specific questions. Oracle cards do not need to be memorized or require any previous understanding. Each one of the cards has a message that is easy to understand and is clearly worded. Reading oracle cards requires no specific skill set. Oracle cards will provide you with guidance and affirmations about what you need to keep in the back of your mind moving forward.

Directions:

1. One the new moon has risen, place your candle in its holder on your altar and light it.
2. Perform some deep breathing exercises and center your thoughts on the goddess Selene.
3. Visualize a glowing white energy force moving up from the top of your head and connecting to the silvery glow of moon goddess Selene.
4. Sense and feel her radiant, cool light descending down from the Moon, even though it isn't visible, and entering your body, filling you completely to the point of it overflowing and illuminating and surroundding your body, like a cocoon of shimmering moonlight.
5. Shuffle your oracle deck of cards.
6. Draw the top four cards and lay them down left to right.
7. The first card will guide you through the first week of the lunar cycle.
8. The second will guide you through the second week, and so on.

9. When you have completed your reading, express your gratitude to the goddess Selene.
10. Place your cards on your altar for review during each week of the lunar cycle.
11. Snuff out your candle.

Adventurous Spell

What You'll Need:

- New moon
- Pen or pencil and paper
- Orange candle
- Orange essential oil
- Cinnamon powder
- Abalone shell
- Sage bundle

Directions:

1. Smudge your lunar altar with sage.
2. Draw a picture of the exact type of activity such as a sport, travel, hobby, sewing, ceramics, wine tasting, etc.
3. Place the picture on your lunar altar.
4. Focus your intention and mind on positive and healthy adventures—you don't want to summon a hurricane.

5. Anoint your candle with the orange essential oil.
6. Light the candle.
7. Speak aloud

   Life is a blast and all is good
   Adventures to last
   Let's run in the woods,
   or make something new,
   or travel abroad.
   To endless adventures, Mother Moon gives a nod.
   So mote it be

8. Sprinkle a pinch of cinnamon into the candle light.
9. Thank Mother Moon and wish her goodnight.

CHAPTER 4:

WAXING CRESCENT MOON SPELLS FOR TAKING ACTION

The waxing crescent moon comes about three to seven days after the new moon, and the main theme is manifestation. A waxing crescent moon is a good time to write down your objectives for the future and to focus and discipline yourself in manifesting your intentions. It is time for preparing for the next set of plans in preparation for the next lunar phase. Potential spells during this period focus on positive energy, attraction and protection magic, healing, wealth, success, friendship, luck, self-improvement, and inner beauty. The waxing crescent moon phase is a time for self-reflection and working toward your future goals and dreams.

Bathe Me in Confidence Spell

Bath magic uses elements like water, salt, and cleaning items—organic shampoos and lavender bath wash—in this ritual, run a bath, add epsom salts or sea salt, light a candle to set the mood, and prepare the environment. After that, take a bath, imagine all your intentions and goals manifesting, think of anything that can hold you back, and let those obstacles flow down the drain as you cleanse yourself physically, emotionally, and spiritually.

Passion Over the Moon Spell

A waxing crescent moon ignites the passions of sensual pleasure and love. Set the scene with your lunar altar dressed in red and pink items. Hang or post pictures of you and your lover, include a couple of magazine pictures with your favorite sexual positions represented. Setting a table with a dozen raw oysters in the half shell won't hurt either. Pour two glasses of burgundy wine, or fruit punch, and put on your favorite soft and sensual music.

What You'll Need:

- Waxing crescent moon
- One red candle
- Jasmine incense
- Wooden bowl
- Cinnamon candies
- 1 cup of rose petals

Directions:

1. Turn the lights down low and open the blinds or curtains if you're inside so you can see the Moon.
2. Put your cinnamon candies on your lunar altar inside the wooden bowl.
3. Stand before your lunar altar and line your rose petals across it while chanting

   Oh Waxing Moon, with love's delight
   With this burning flame, let passions ignite.
4. Light the red candle.
5. Light the jasmine incense and take in its aroma.

6. Spend a moment in the aroma, gazing at the candle, and building your feelings of passion.
7. Suck on some of the cinnamon candy, imagining it filling you with passion and joy.
8. Turn up the music and dance under the moon

Grant Me Patience Spell

What You'll Need:

- Waxing crescent moon
- Howlite crystal
- Six blue tea lights
- Paper
- Blue pen
- Sigil for patience. You can copy and draw the sigil here and and put it on your lunar altar for the spell.

Directions:

1. Cleanse your area for the lunar ritual, including your altar. Make sure all items are charged.

2. Draw your sigil. The sigil above symbolizes *patience*.
3. Write "patience" on a piece of paper or something like, "I am patient."
4. Put your howlite crystal on top of your sigil and written word(s).
5. Light the six blue tea lights around the sigil and crystal
6. Hold both hands together over the top of the howlite and say aloud.

   My impatience has now come to an end
   My ability to wait and my attitude to bend
   I ask Mother Moon, for her patience to send
   I will calmly wait for her to attend
   So mote it be

7. Bury your drawing and words on paper under the Waxing Crescent Moon.
8. Let your candles burn down or snuff them out to close the spell.

I Made the First Move Spell

If you are going to make the first move on a love interest, you first want to tell yourself out loud how you are absolutely desirable and a good catch. This spell is more powerful if you take the time to give yourself a makeover. Practicing a little self-love enhances any spell. Try changing your hairstyle, getting a new outfit, and generally inviting positive and new energies into your life.

What You'll Need:

- Waxing crescent moon
- A red tapered candle
- Tea tree incense
- Clear quartz crystal

Directions:

1. Smudge your space and charge your clear quartz crystal—smudging charges the crystal.
2. Light your tea tree incense to enhance your sexual energy for making that first move.
3. Point your crystal to the west for confidence and romantic desirability.
4. Place your red tapered candle in the center of your lunar altar and light it.

   May I be seen as wonderful today
   Give me the confidence to make my way
   The reception is grand, I'm seen in good light
   Under the Moon, my first move's delight
   As it is and should be

5. Visualize the crystal pulling the energy from the waxing crescent moon into your candle looping around, flowing through you, and shining bright.

6. Let the candle burn down, and thank the Mother Moon for responding to you.
7. Put the crystal in your pocket or purse and carry it with you when you make the first move.
8. Keep it with you until your desires are met.

Conflict Resolution Spell

What You'll Need:
- Waxing crescent moon
- Moon-blessed water
- Pen and paper
- 2 pink round candles
- A large enough mirror to place on your lunar altar and hold candles
- A picture of you and the person with whom you are in conflict. If you don't have a picture of the person(s) involved write your name and theirs on a piece of paper.

Directions:
1. Cleanse your sacred space.
2. Place both candles side by side on top of the mirror.
3. Light the candles focusing your mind on the words *peace* and *harmony*.

4. Draw a heart around the picture of you and the person.
5. Write the words "peace" and "harmony" on the back of the picture or paper.
6. Speak the following mantra out loud three times

   This conflict is clouding my heart and my mind
   Cause no more distress, let's all be kind.
   Themis, Pasithea, shall sanctify
   Love and peace Mother Moon will amplify.
   So mote it be.

7. Set the picture and paper aflame and let them burn all the way on top of the mirror.
8. Take a few drops of moon-blessed water and mix it into the ashes.
9. Form a heart with the wet ashes.
10. Thank the Moon Goddess.
11. Let the heart dry overnight.
12. Dig a small hole in the dirt and bury the ashes, along with any conflict and resentments you may feel.
13. Take the mirror off the lunar altar. It did its job by multiplying the power of the candles and reflecting the Moon's vibrational energies into your spell.

Energy Cleansing Ritual

What You'll Need:

- Waxing crescent moon
- Cinnamon stick
- Clear quartz crystal
- White candle
- Paper and pen

Direction:

1. Write a list of any negative forces in your life that you are ready to release on a piece of paper.
2. Fold the paper up and put it on your lunar altar in front of you.
3. Light your candle.
4. Hold your cinnamon stick in the flame until it starts smoking.
5. Trace the lines of your body with the cinnamon stick smoke, over and around your head, down to your shoulders, around your arms and torso, down and around your legs, back, and over your feet. You may have to keep relighting your cinnamon stick, if you have no luck at all getting the cinnamon stick to smoke, place it on your altar and complete those steps with a sage or palo alto bundle.

6. While gazing in the flame of your candle, slow your thinking and relax your mind. Spend a full 60 seconds taking the deepest breaths you can in through your nose and into your belly before releasing it out through your mouth.
7. Visualize all and any negativity forming into a black cloud of smoke billowing up from your deepest core as you are slowly breathing in and being forced from your body and your surroundings—with the force of your exhale—out into the atmosphere, past the earth, and disintegrated by the Moon.
8. Repeat steps 6 and 7 until it feels tangible and real.
9. Be done with the list on your paper by burning it thoroughly.
10. Thank the goddesses and gods of the Moon for a thorough deep cleansing.
11. Notice how light you feel on your feet and smile.

Enemy Protection Spell

What You'll Need:

- Waxing crescent moon
- A black candle
- A white candle
- Lavender and rose essential oils
- 4 small glass jars
- Dried lemon peel, basil, black salt, and rice.

Directions:

1. On the morning of the true waxing crescent moon, smudge your house in its entirety.
2. Fill each of the four jars with the dried lemon peels, basil, and black salt. You can make the black salt by mixing the ashes from your sage bundle with the white sea salt.
3. Place them on your lunar altar or on a windowsill where they can absorb the Moon's energy.
4. Place them in a diamond pattern to represent the four cardinal directions. The lavender will bring you peace and the basil and black salt will ward off and protect you from your enemies. The rice brings you good luck and the lemon boosts the powers of each ingredient.

5. Let them charge under the waxing crescent moon overnight.
6. The next day, in the morning, place one candle in between the jars on your altar.
7. Anoint your candles with the lavender and rose oils.
8. Light the black candle to banish evil and protect you from any enemies.
9. Light the white candle to purify your thoughts and your environment.
10. With your intentions set in clarity, cast your spell:

    Protect this house from from danger and dirt
    Get rid of my enemies plans to hurt
    Fill me with strength and the power to see
    And anything harmful aimed at me
    So mote it be

11. Let both candles burn down completely and then bury the wax under the Moon in your yard.
12. Keep the jars on your altar until the next lunar phase.
13. Pour the contents of the jars into an abalone shell and spread them around the outskirts of your home to ward off your enemies.

CHAPTER 5:

FIRST QUARTER MOON SPELLS FOR MAKING DECISIONS

The first quarter moon looks like a half pie, and it is a time to face the obstacles and challenges in your path, to focus on the elements that matter in this phase and on reaching your goals. Other spells that work during this phase include creative magic, such as divination, growth, motivation, and strength. During the first quarter moon phase, visualization is a great way to get creative with your lunar magic. Start out with simple lunar meditations, visualizing your intentions for this particular lunar phase.

Also, for this particular lunar phase, practice your breathing with the full intention of relaxing. Breathe deep into your belly and slowly exhale. Deep breathing can reset the mind and body. Studies have revealed that deep breathing restores balance to the central nervous system and the body's stress response, calms agitation, and lowers anxiety levels (Brown & Gerbarg, 2012). Breathe in and count to four, and then hold your breath and count to four, and exhale counting to four 4-4-4, it's easy.

First Quarter Ritual Idea

Sacred Water Ritual

What You'll Need:
- First quarter moon
- Glass of spring water
- Natural salt
- A burned piece of incense

Directions:

1. Put the salt and the incense into the glass of water.
2. Place the glass in the center of your lunar altar and start the ritual.
3. Mediate and review your special intentions.

Healthy Habits Spell

The first quarter moon is in transition between a new and full moon. It is a time for refinement and adjustment. Health wise, nutritional challenges may occur and you may find yourself struggling to eat healthy. Keep a positive mindset and treat yourself kindly. It is a good time for readjusting your health goals and maybe upping the ante and challenging yourself a bit more. Maybe cut down on your alcohol or caffeine intake, or shop for organic foods.

Note: The color corresponding with a first quarter moon is yellow, and its incense is poplar.

What You'll Need:

- First quarter moon
- Light blue cloth
- An apple
- A light blue candle

- Poplar incense
- Rose essential oil

DIRECTIONS

1. On the evening of the first quarter moon
2. Cleanse your lunar altar
3. Anoint your light blue candle with the rose essential oil
4. Light your incense
5. Slice your apple in half to represent the moon.
6. Chant the following aloud.

   Mother Moon, I'm here to say
   I believe in an apple a day.
   Half for me and half for you
   I'll wrap your half in a very light blue.
   Bring to me healthy habits to stay
   I feel them filling me with your light blue rays.
   So mote it be.

7. Eat your half of the apple
8. Wrap the other half of the apple in the blue cloth
9. Bury the blue cloth containing the half apple in the ground under the moon.
10. Thank Mother Moon and snuff out your candle to close the spell.

Mental Clarity Spell

This spell is best cast during a first quarter moon and using items that correspond with the element air.

What You'll Need:

- First quarter moon
- Yellow candle
- Feathers
- Lemons
- Cardamon
- Lemongrass incense
- Pen and paper
- A bowl of clear spring water
- Scissors

Directions:

1. Cleanse your lunar altar
2. Adorn your altar with feathers, lemons, cardamom, and any items that resonate with you and correspond with the element air.
3. Carve or scribe this sigil for mental clarity in your yellow candle:

4. Put your bowl of water in front of your candle in the center of your lunar altar.
5. Light your yellow candle and speak out loud

   I call upon the Moon Goddess to ask for your help.
   Remove my distractions, give clarity to myself.
   Oh thank you, oh Moon, for healing my mind.
   All mental distractions are now left behind.
   As it is and should be.

6. Relax your mind and meditate on your bowl of water
7. As thoughts come into your mind, jot them down and then release them from your mind.
8. After each thought has come and gone, refocus on your water bowl and your candle. If any intrusive thoughts enter your mind, fan them away with a feather.
9. Meditate and continue the ritual for thirty minutes, a *full* thirty minutes or longer, until your mind is clear.
10. Look at your list and then cut the page so that each item is on its own strip of paper.
11. Starting with the least important item, burn them one by one, visualizing the smoke on its way to the moon.

12. Thank the Moon Goddess and either snuff or let your candle burn all the way down to close the spell.

Make the Right Decision Spell

Your subconscious mind is governed by the moon; that part of yourself that is felt at the deepest soulful level and is often the part most difficult to express. Using the lunar energetic shift as a roadmap for planning your goals will help you manifest decisions for living your best life. Afterall, the word lunatic, which now means crazy, first meant deep lovers of the moon. With the first quarter moon, you are able to move toward implementing your new moon intentions. In other words, now is the time for decision making. Use this phase of the Moon's momentum to overcome any obstacles you may be facing along the way. You can change and add things that need to be readjusted with the intentions you have for the new moon during the first quarter moon phase. The gods and goddesses of the Universe are allowing you to edit your intentions according to your needs and lifestyle.

What You'll Need:

- First quarter moon
- Pen and paper

- An old key

Directions:

1. Cleanse your lunar altar.
2. Draw the capital letter Y on a piece of paper to symbolize a fork in the road.

3. You are calling upon the powers of the Maiden aspect of the Moon. At night during the first quarter moon—just before you go to bed—place the old key that you don't need anymore over the letter Y on your altar and speak three times:

   I have decisions to make
   Tell me which path to take.
   With this key my mind straightens
   To seek the wisdom of the Maiden.
   So mote it be.

4. Go straight to bed. You will either awaken with your answer or you will dream prophetically.

Pivot Spell

Everything doesn't always go the way we want it to, or the way we think it is going to go. Sometimes life takes a sudden turn in the wrong direction, and you can either change course entirely or take a step back and get back on track. Whichever path you decide to take, the best thing you can do is enjoy the scenery. This spell will help you to pivot and enjoy the scenery, either way you turn.

What You'll Need:

- First quarter moon
- Light blue candle
- Tongs
- Small piece of blue paper
- Blue ink pen
- White paper
- Black paper
- Fireproof container or cauldron
- Blue attire
- Frankincense

Directions:

1. One one side of the small piece of blue paper, write down the path or direction you have been heading.

2. On the other side of the small blue piece of paper, write down an obstacle or struggle that has revealed itself to you, requiring you to make a pivotal decision.
3. Place the blue paper with your writings in between the white and black paper.
4. Form a makeshift folder out of the papers by bending the edges together, holding the blue paper in between them.
5. Light the papers on fire over your blue candle, using tongs for safety.
6. Speak the following out loud.

   First quarter moon, show me the way.
   So I may pivot accordingly today.
   So mote it be.

7. After the ashes have cooled, take them outside and toss them toward the Moon.
8. Let your candle burn or snuff it out, thank Mother Moon and close the spell.

To Tell the Truth

What You'll Need:

- First quarter moon
- White candle
- Cauldron or fireproof container
- Lighter or matches

- A strand of the person's hair you want to speak the truth
- Pen and paper

Directions:

1. Place your white candle in the center of your lunar altar
2. Write the name or names of the people from whom you are seeking the truth
3. Place the strand of hair in the piece of paper with their name(s) on it and fold it closed before placing it in the cauldron and speak the following out loud.

   First quarter moon, help me now.
   I seek the truth yet to be found.
   For under your magic today there lies
   The truth to be told to open my eyes.
   Your magic is strong and like no other
   To have this person show their true colors.
   So mote it be.

4. Burn the paper in your cauldron while focusing on the flame and your intention.
5. Let the paper burn all the way to ash.
6. Thank Mother Moon and close the spell.

CHAPTER 6:
WAXING GIBBOUS MOON SPELLS FOR GETTING SPECIFIC

A waxing gibbous moons feels more energetic; it is a time to tie up loose ends, develop, and achieve your desired results. Spellwise, it's a time for constructive magic.

Waxing Gibbous Ritual

What You'll Need:

- Waxing gibbous moon
- A yellow candle
- A star anise
- 2 pinches of dried rosemary
- Mortar and pestle

Directions:

1. Blend your frankincense, star anise, and dried rosemary with your mortar and pestle.
2. Place the blend in a small jar or herb container in the middle of your lunar altar.
3. Light your yellow candle.
4. Focus your intention into the flame and speak the following out loud.

   Oh Maiden Moon, hear my plea.
   Listen please unto me.
   As you grow, my spells enhance.
   Under your light, my magic will dance.
   Speak to me with clear and loud signs.
   Let me share in your great Maiden mind.
   So mote it be.

Personification Spell

When we see the waxing gibbous moon rising in the night, it is the goddess Selene waving hello from her chariot of silver drawn by two white horses. Selene is the personification of the moon itself, and her powers correspond with intuition, dreams, emotions, healing, and much more.

What You'll Need:

- A picture of the waxing gibbous moon
- Two moonstone crystals, symbolizing Selene
- Any type of horse figurines, especially in white or silver if possible.
- Moon-blessed water
- A silver bowl
- A handwritten by you poem dedicated to Selene
- Cleansed bathtub
- Rose petals
- A silver or white robe

Directions:

1. Cleanse your lunar altar with sage and dedicate your sacred altar to Selene. Tell her you built it in her honor.
2. Place your moonstones and blessed water on the altar.

3. Read your poem out loud to her.
4. Fill your silver bowl with the moon-blessed water
5. Prepare a bath and float your rose petals
6. Pour your moon-blessed water from the silver bowl into the tub
7. Speak the following out loud.

   Goddess of the Moon, Selene, may your love and moonlight fill my needs.
   I see you personified
   In love and the water's tides.
   Connect me to you, for you are so wise.
   So mote it be.

8. Take a ritual bath in honor of Selene, the goddess of the Moon.
9. Wear a silver robe in her honor for the rest of the night.

Communication Spell

Crystals harness the power of the waxing gibbous moon; specifically, lapis lazuli is known as the "stone of truth." It helps you to communicate clearly, honestly, and effectively both with yourself and with others. Its name comes from the Persian and Latin word meaning "blue stone." Blue is also the color of the throat chakra, which corresponds with your abilities for expressing yourself. It is also a protective gem against the negative thoughts and words of others. Adding clear quartz and amethyst to your lunar altar while charging your lapis lazuli with moon-blessed water will boot the spell's energy. It is always good to keep a few gallons of moon-blessed water around, and you can even freeze it to make ice cubes.

What You'll Need:

- Waxing gibbous moon
- A piece lapis lazuli
- A amethyst
- 1 or more clear quartz crystals
- A yellow or white candle

Directions:

1. Cleanse your lunar altar.
2. Place the clear quartz crystal and the amethyst crystal in front of your yellow or white candle and light the candle.
3. Hold the lapis lazuli cupped in both hands.
4. Close your eyes and deep breathe.
5. Visualize the moonbeams shooting down from the sky and into the lapis lazuli.
6. Picture yourself feeling satisfied and relieved about how easy it is for you to have a conversation.

7. See the positive energy flowing from the Moon into the crystal and through your hands while saying the following out loud three times.

   I communicate effectively and clearly from the essence of truth.
   My conversations will no longer seem aloof.
   So mote it be.

8. When you feel the energy has fully charged the crystal, place it near the clear quartz and amethyst crystals and leave all three there with the candle burning for at least two hours.

9. Keep the lapis lazuli stone with you, where it will be ready to help you with your conversations.

Positivity Spell Jar

Jasmine flowers are known to absorb and infuse many energies—lunar magic, friendship, spiritual connections, and so much more.

What You'll Need:

- Waxing gibbous moon
- Jar that has been charged in moonlight to remove any negative energies.

- A white candle for balance and harmony.
- 4 grams of jasmine flowers
- 4 grams chamomile flowers
- 4 grams pink himalayan salt
- 4 grams sunflower petals for protection and energy
- 4 grams of rose petals for domestic happiness
- 4 grams of sea salt for cleansing and protection
- 4 grams coffee grounds for positive energy and peace
- 4 grams cinnamon for protection
- 4 grams ginger for prosperity and positivity
- 4 grams cloves for protection
- 4 grams vanilla beans for positivity and energy

Directions:

1. Focus on the attributes of each item as you put them in your jar. The attributes are listed next to the ingredients above.
2. Layer them according to your intuition.
3. Seal the jar with wax or tightly with the lip.
4. Place your hands over the lid.
5. Say the following out loud three times.

   Mother Moon, bless this jar with happiness, protection, energy, and positivity.
   So mote it be.

6. Meditate under the waxing gibbous moon, letting its energy flow into the jar.
7. Feel your energy, charged from the moon, flowing through your hands into the lid and into the jar.
8. Snuff out your candle and close the spell.
9. Keep the jar on your lunar altar until the next lunar phase, then keep it somewhere that you can see it often, filling you with positivity the way you filled it.

Inspirational Moon Spell

Spells for inspiration can help your creativity and motivation start flowing with the life of the moonlit stars. This spell will provide you with the inspiration for starting something you have been dreaming of—or inspire new motivation for a project or situation you are already in the middle of doing.

Sometimes you need a little additional energy to get inspiration going, and this simple spell uses some fire to make that happen.

What You'll Need:
- Waxing gibbous moon
- Yellow candle
- Flame proof container or surface

- Two dry sprigs of mint

Directions:

1. Light your yellow candle and speak the following out loud.

   Fuse and spark ignite my heart
   In its fuse, find my muse
   Within its flame, inspiration untamed
   Smoke in the air, time to care and take a dare
   So mote it be.

2. Hole a mint sprig in your right hand and light it in the flame of your yellow candle.
3. Hold them out in front of your lunar altar.
4. As they smolder and the smoke rises toward Mother Moon, repeat the chant two more times.
5. Let the ashes fall into your abalone shell.
6. Take the ashes outside and toss them toward the Moon, visualizing her dancing around and collecting each piece while she returns your worship with inspiration.
7. Snuff your candle and express your gratitude to the moon goddess of inspiration and close the spell.

Reclaim Personal Power Spell

This spell is a recovery ritual for reclaiming your personal power. It provides you with the ability to identify all of the times where situations and people zapped your powers and energy and allows you to reclaim them. There is not ill intent or anger involved in this ritual, it simply helps you to look at the past few months to a year and reclaim the personal power that is rightfully yours

The waxing gibbous moon will guide you to a place of neutrality, so you can come to understand that providing people your anger is giving them power over you. It affords you a place of neutrality, so if need be, repeat the spell as often as necessary as a training exercise.

What You'll Need:

- Waxing gibbous moon
- Two bowls
- Two red candles as red corresponds with power
- A collection of small items
    - pebbles
    - small crystals
    - beads
    - leaves

- Moon incense
- Pen and paper

Directions:

1. Set up your lunar altar with one candle to the left and one to the right.
2. Place your two bowls in a straight line, one close to you and one further away.
3. Fill the bowl furthest from you with your small items—not the pen and paper.
4. The items in the bowl furthest from you represent your energetic powers that you will be working toward returning them to you, so make sure you have plenty of these small items.
5. Light your moon incense and your candles.
6. Find your stillness through breathing and relaxing.
7. You are creating a sacred space for safety, comfort, and renewal.
8. Meditate on retrieving your personal powers. Feel the magic of the waxing gibbous moon's healing energy
9. Write down the circumstances causing you the need to reclaim your powers. Write down specifically where you think they are hiding.

10. Reach into the bowl with your items—the one furthest away—and pick one item.
11. Hold it in your hand and name the person, situation, or moment that you are reclaiming your energy and power from. For instance, "I am taking my power back from_____"
12. Place the item in the closest bowl to you and concentrate on feeling its energy, fueled by the moon, rushing back and filling you with power.
13. Continue until you have reclaimed all of your power and transferred each item.
14. You can take a break and go back to transferring items if you start to feel fatigued. This spell needs to be cast after a good night's sleep, or after you have taken a nap on the day of the waxing gibbous moon.

Prosperity Spell

Using the waxing gibbous moon for prosperity is like turning on a powerful magnet for good luck. Do the work on your part and Mother Moon will respond with prosperity like you have never seen before.

What You'll Need:

- Waxing gibbous moon

- Anthem or a penknife
- A green candle
- Green aventurine, the prosperity stone
- Green citrine for positivity

Directions:

1. Carve or scribe the exact type of prosperity or amount of money you wish to manifest on the side of your green candle. Make it something within your reach.
2. Place the candle in the middle of your lunar altar and light it.
3. Place the green citrine and the green aventurine on each side of your candle
4. Light your candle and spend a few moments with the image in your mind of how your life will change with great prosperity as if it has already happened.
5. Blow the candle out.
6. Relight the candle and conduct the ritual every night at the same time while the moon is waxing.
7. By the end of the week, you will see things starting to change for the better.

Strengthen My Love Spell

Faithfulness and trust are complex and inborn needs. Love relationships require mutual respect and compromise. Usually, when there is a weakness in a relationship, it is due to one or both of the individual's insecurities. For this spell, you will be using crystals to harness the waxing gibbous moon's energy to strengthen you and your loved one's bond.

What You'll Need:

- Waxing gibbous moon
- Poppy seeds
- Rosemary
- Cardamom
- Sodalite
- Lapis lazuli
- A dark blue or black drawstring pouch

Directions:

1. Scatter one-half of the poppy seeds over your lover's footprints.
2. Put the rest of the poppy seeds in the pouch.
3. Add some cardamom to a meal you are enjoying together at the same time.
4. Hold a lapis lazuli crystal in one hand and the sodalite crystal in the other hand.

5. Close your eyes and chant the following out loud.

   I trust our love; our bond is true.
   Under this moon, our love strengthens too.
   Our love is one that time cannot cheat.
   It's strong and powerful, no challenge can beat.
   So mote it be.

6. Put all of the ingredients in the pouch and place it on your lunar altar until the next lunar cycle. Repeat the spell each waxing gibbous moon phase until you feel the spell is complete.

CHAPTER 7:

FULL MOON SPELLS FOR CELEBRATION, GLOW, AND REFLECTION

Full moons attract all good things to you and heal you from the past emotional pains. It can be constructive and destructive, banishing unwanted energies and influences from your life, performing divination magic, creating protection spells.

Full Moon Ritual Idea for divination and reading. It is a time to communicate with spirits and deities. Sit down with a view of the full moon and start a ritual meditation. Concentrate on your intentions and on receiving guidance from the goddess, and after you're done, you need to ground yourself. Eating something heavy helps with this.

Smoke Cleansing Ritual

What You'll Need:
- Full moon
- Sage
- Palo santo

Directions:

1. Ceremoniously cleanse away any negative energies hanging around you, your home, and your electronic devices.

Note: Palo santo and white sage are at risk of over-harvesting due to their popularity and face the potential for extinction. Try growing your own sage to make bundles and source responsibly.

Dream Vision Spell

What You'll Need:

- Full moon
- Blue ink pen
- Small piece of white paper
- Clear quartz crystal
- White round candle

Directions:

1. Cleanse your lunar altar
2. Decorate your altar with any items and written symbols that honor the full moon.
3. Carve a question mark into the candle.
4. Place your candle in the middle of your altar.
5. Place your four clear quartz crystals symbolizing the cardinal directions.
6. Light your white candle.
7. Write down a question you desire the answer for, and it can be regarding anything occupying your thoughts.
8. Fold it in half and speak the following out loud.

Mother Moon Goddess, as I travel the astral realm,
I wish to know [speak your question].

My will be done.
So mote it be.

9. Leave the piece of paper folded under the candle overnight, make sure the candle is in a safe place to burn and let it burn while you sleep, and you will awaken with your answer.

Ritual Steps for Harvesting Full Moon Bliss

1. Turn off all devices.
2. Breathe six long breaths in silence under the full moon, where you have a clear view of it.
3. Focus on the full moon's cleansing effects.
4. Light a white candle and a blue candle. This is best if you can make an outdoor lunar altar. This will enhance your intuition and help you to release all negativity.
5. Write with a blue pen on white paper any of your troubles. For instance, problems with addiction, bad situations, or even a negative person in your life. Writing things down makes your intentions for harvesting a blissful life much more clear.
6. Visualize your blissfulness. Picture your life being blissful. Let your soul swell with blissfulness the full moon offers you.

7. Ask the Mother Moon for forgiveness out loud. This mantra is for forgiving someone else or yourself.

   I forgive myself or [person's/institution/ etc.]
   So mote it be.

8. Feel all of the negativity leave your body as your chakras align with the full moon.
9. Express your gratitude and close the spell.

Lunar Rejuvenation Spell

What You'll Need:

- Full moon
- Rose quartz crystal
- Light purple altar cloth
- Celestial music, there are many ethereal soundtracks available free online
- Athame
- Moon incense or jasmine incense
- A glass of wine or punch
- Shot glass or small cup
- Velvet drawstring pouch in dark blue or black

Directions:

1. Take a ritual cleansing bath.
2. Cleanse your lunar altar.
3. Cast your circle around your altar.

4. Light your moon or jasmine incense and charge your crystal with the smoke. Ask your crystal to harness the energy of the full moon and bring it to you.
5. Sit on the ground and enter into a meditative state, checking your body for all emotional awareness. It feels like a tugging sense or a heaviness.
6. Symbolize severing your mind and body from that heaviness with your anthem. Remember this is symbolic, be very careful to hold your anthem far from your body.
7. Visualize the full moon's light pulsating over you.
8. Visualize the full moon's glow entering into your body, telling you, "you are alive!"
9. Pick up your crystal and visualize the Moon's remaining energy drawn into it.
10. Place the crystal in the bag and carry it with you, looking at it every evening under the full moon throughout this lunar phase.
11. Toast your glass of wine or punch to the Mother Moon and tell her out loud how rejuvenated you feel.
12. Pour a small amount of wine into a cup or shot glass and place it on your altar.
13. Open the circle and the spell is completed.

Self-Love Celebration Spell

What You'll Need:

- Pen or marker
- A leaf from outside
- Purple candle
- Lighter
- Rose quartz crystals
- Pink altar cloth
- Sage
- Fireproof glass or mirror

Directions:

1. Turn off and unplug anything not involved in your full moon magic.
2. Create a sacred space with your lunar altar in the middle outside under the full moon.
3. Smudge all of your items, yourself, and your sacred space.
4. Light your purple candle
5. Make sure you are under the full moon and that it is shining down on your space. If it's raining, open all of your curtains and set your altar close to the window.
6. On your fallen leaf, write down what you want to release and what you want to attract.
7. On a piece of paper write three affirmations:

"I am strong."
"I am beautiful."
"I am wise."
"I am happy with who I am."
"I love me."

8. Speak each affirmation out loud.
9. Burn the paper and visualize the full moon inhaling the smoke and returning to you in the form of a hugging sensation encircling your entire body.
10. Burn the leaf.
11. Take the ashes from the leaf and throw them in the air, visualizing Mother Moon and Mother Nature together, telling you to love and care for yourself the way they do.

CHAPTER 8:
WANING GIBBOUS MOON SPELLS FOR EXPRESSING GRATITUDE

A waning gibbous moon means a decrease in anything negative or unneeded. Its magic is good for banishing spells, cleaning up your living space, cleaning magic, removing curses, cleansing spells, undoing bindings, and removing negativity.

Waning Gibbous Ritual Idea

Write down a list of all your fears, troubles, insecurities. For this ritual, you can burn the paper while surrendering to the moon's power as you banish and relinquish those doubts, and move toward getting what you need and deserve.

Embracing Obstacles Spell

What You'll Need:

- Waning gibbous moon
- A small, hand-held mirror
- An acorn or some other type of berry or nut that has fallen from a tree
- A piece of yarn tied in a loose knot
- A black candle

Directions:

1. Cleanse your lunar altar.
2. Place your mirror in the middle of your altar.
3. Place your knotted yarn and berry in the middle of your mirror.
4. Light your candle.

5. Speak the following out loud.

   Mirror, Mirror, on my Altar,
   Bless me Moon so I won't falter.
   Obstacles come and then they go.
   My inner strength is all I know.
   So mote it be.

6. Pick up your yarn, untie the knot, and place it back on your altar.
7. Take the acorn or berry and bury it in the back yard or somewhere close to your dwelling.
8. Look at yourself in the mirror and repeat the chant.
9. Snuff out your candle and close the spell.

Honor Thy Anger Spell

What You'll Need:

- A black candle
- A red candle
- A white candle
- A light blue candle
- A small, white tea candle

Directions:

1. Place all four candles on your lunar altar with the small white tea candle in the middle.

2. Light your candles and say the following out loud five times.

   Anger is reality.
   Anger is protection.
   Anger is human.
   Anger is a message from the Universe.
   Anger is energy.
   Anger is power.

3. Blow out the tea candle and let the other four burn for one hour.
4. After the hour is up, snuff the candles out and close the spell.

Honoring a Relationship Spell

What You'll Need:

- Waning gibbous moon
- Two bundles of parsley
- A white thread
- A red Candle
- 2 lighters

Directions:

1. Sit together with your partner under a waning gibbous moon.
2. Each of you strike your lighters and light the candle together.

3. Each of you wrap the string around the base of the parsley nine times
4. Both of you pick up the bundle of parsley you each wrapped.
5. Stand facing each other.
6. While you are passing your parsley bundles to each other, tell each other three things you are grateful for in the relationship.
7. Lay the parsley bundle you received next to you on the altar
8. Let the candle burn all the way in a safe place, or snuff it out while holding hands and complete the spell.

Thanksgiving Ritual During Waning Gibbous Moon

What You'll Need:
- Waning Gibbous Moon
- Chair
- Orange candle
- Jasmine incense
- Pen and paper

Directions:
1. Create Sacred Space and light the orange candle and the jasmine incense.

2. Write down what you are grateful for, including qualities you like in yourself, your achievements, your obstacles, for being free, for Mother Moon, and for your family.
3. List your intentions for the next lunar phase.
4. Sit on the chair and connect with the Moon in meditation. Visualize yourself like you are a flower, opening up to the Moon, and the Moon is watering you with its silver light.
5. Read out loud through your gratitude list and think about the feelings associated with each item. The words are the framework holding together the energy you are manifesting for the ritual. Focus intently on conjuring up emotions of gratitude. This opens up channels for the Moon's magic to infiltrate your spirit.
6. Sit for thirty minutes with this feeling, let it overflow you with happiness and joy.
7. Set an intention for the good of someone else.
8. Thank the Moon, Mother Earth, the Elements, and any other celestial beings you can think of.
9. Snuff the candle and close the ritual.

Minimalism Moon Spell

Directions:

1. Pick eleven days and take notice of the number eleven everywhere you go.
2. Keep a journal of everything you have seen with the number eleven involved.
3. When you see 11 11 or 1 you will know your intuition is elevated.

Thanking Mother Earth Spell

What You'll Need:

- Waning gibbous moon
- Garden soil
- Bowl
- Dried leaves
- Coffee grounds
- A green or brown candle
- A blue candle
- A yellow candle
- Spring water in a spouted container

Directions:

1. Place your garden soil in the bowl on your outdoor lunar altar
2. Add in your coffee grounds and mix together well.
3. Draw a river or jungle path with your finger through the dirt

4. Inscribe your blue candle with the Laguz rune symbol for water and Ansuz rune symbol for air.

5. Inscribe your brown candle with the Inguz the rune symbol for earth

6. Inscribe your yellow candle with Kenaz, the rune symbol for fire

7. Add your spring water.
8. Say out loud

   Mother Earth holds the water.
   It's healing blue.
   She holds the sand
   and heals the land

with all that's green.
Please bless her, Mother Moon
with all that is clean.
So mote it be.

9. Stir the water into the dirt
10. Continue chanting until the soil is mixed and damp.
11. Sprinkle some of the soil onto the Earth to carry your spell's intention.
12. Keep the soil mixture on your altar in a sealed container.
13. Whenever you see something unkind to nature, sprinkle some of the dirt either where it happened or symbolically in your own yard.

CHAPTER 9:
WANING CRESCENT MOON FOR SURRENDER AND RELEASE

A waning crescent moon is a time of restoration, healing, meditating, and nurturing yourself. Use it to recuperate, rest, and recharge your energy. This phase will help you find balance and slow down to reflect on the past and help you to resolve any struggles so you may move forward.

Dark Goddess Ritual

What You'll Need:

- Three black candles
- Lighter
- Ash or soot, you can use your incense or sage ash for extra *umph*
- Hand mirror
- Black obsidian crystal
- Homemade cookies or fresh flowers, I like making the cookies
- Offerings for the goddess
- Witch's wand

Directions:

1. Cleanse your lunar altar with sage and keep the ash.
2. Place your black obsidian crystal on the mirror
3. Surround the mirror and the crystal with the candles
4. Light your three black candles and notice the reflection of the black candles as representing the dark goddess.
5. Speak the following out loud.

   I invoke you, Dark Goddess of the Moon, into my sacred space to grant me the power of compassion and to instill upon me a deep knowledge of divine magic. I ask that you illuminate my journey. So mote it be.

6. Collect the ash in your abalone shell.
7. Hold the shell up to the sky and say the chant again.
8. Toss the ash in the air and visualize the dark goddess reaching with very long arms dressed in black silk to gather the ash and return a silver streak of light enveloping your mind, your body, and your soul.
9. Snuff your candles and close the spell.

Banish My Alcohol Addiction Spell

What You'll Need:

- Waning crescent moon
- A black candle
- A white candle
- Totem (fingernails, toenails, lock of hair, or something they have worn on their body) of the person if it is not you.
- Pen and paper

Directions:

1. Place the white candle in the center of your lunar altar.
2. Place the black candle on the west side of the white candle
3. Place the totem next to the white candle on the east side.
4. Write down the exact outcome you desire as if it has already occurred.

   I did not drink today.
   I did not drink one day at a time.
   I am healthy.
   I am nourished.
   Mother Moon, banish my desire for alcohol.
   So mote it be.

5. Tear the paper up in thirteen pieces.

6. Place the crumbled pieces of paper in a row heading west from the black candle.
7. Light both candles, visualizing what a clean and sober life would be. Feel the freedom from your vice picture the happiness in your loved ones.
8. Burn the first crumbled paper nearest to the black candle.
9. Move the black candle over the space where the burned paper sat away from the white candle.
10. For thirteen nights, burn one piece and move the cande. Continue until all of the crumbled pieces are burned and the black candle is far away from the white candle.
11. Notice you have thirteen days sober.
12. Repeat the entire ritual for as long as you need.

You Need to Cut the Cord Spell

What You'll Need:
- Waning crescent moon
- 3 Pieces of yarn — red, white, and blue
  - Red: the connection and passion that binds you

- White: your willingness and intention to bring the situation to light.
- Blue: welcoming the knowledge during and after the ritual.

- A white candle
- A bowl of water
- A white sage bundle
- Scissors

Directions:

1. Sit outside under the moon where you will have zero interruptions.
2. Place the white candle on your outdoor lunar altar in front of you. If you can find a tree stump or a flat rock, it would enhance your mood and therefore your magic.
3. Meditate on the white candle, symbolizing divine pure light. It mirrors the flame and harnesses the energy of the waning crescent moon.
4. Visualize your intentions passing through the flame, guided by the Moon's vibrational energy.
5. Light your sage bundle and smudge yourself, your altar, and the area around you.
6. Make three, 9-inch sections of yarn in red, white, and blue with the scissors, symbolizing cutting the cord.

7. Braid the three strands of yarn and tie a small knot at the ends.
8. Clear your mind, harness the Moon's infinite power, and pour all of your raw energy and intention into the braided cord.
9. Say out loud

    It is my intention to cut the cord.
    It's this relationship I cannot afford.
    It's time for me to cut all ties.
    It's time for me to say goodbye.
    I feel this with all of my might.
    Please fill the space with your gorgeous moonlight.
    So mote it be.

10. While you are holding the strands, put all of your questions, feelings, and frustrations into the cord.
11. Let any anger and sadness you feel rise inside of you meet your intention, including the shedding of tears, knowing they are released and cannot hijack your being any longer.
12. Sit holding the cord until you have released all pent up emotions and are left with a sense of utter relaxation.
13. Say the following out loud.

    I have let you go.
    This you should know.

The cord is cut.
This pathway is shut.
For me, for you, I forgive.
With peace in my heart, I can now live.
So mote it be.

14. Allow the cord to burn in the candle flame.
15. Dip your hands in the now moon-blessed water and shake them dry, symbolizing good riddance.
16. Smudge yourself again after the ritual
17. Put out the candle and go in peace.

FINAL THOUGHTS

It is no surprise the Wiccans, witches, and pagans love the Moon—and so does most of humanity. Hopefully, you have learned a great deal about how to harness the powers of the lunar phases and in the process how to elevate all of your spells with her magic. Throughout this book, the one constant other than the Moon itself, is the importance of your lunar altar. It is specifically dedicated to each phase of the Moon with corresponding items, colors, herbs, candles, crystals, and essential oils.

One of the many topics covered in *Moon Spells: Your Complete Guide to the Hidden Power of Lunar Phases, Wiccan Magic, Rituals, and Witchcraft* is that our internal biological rhythms are connected to Moon's cycle. Gaining an intimate relationship with the Moon and her energies is essential to any witchcraft practice. If she can control the tides of the great waters on Earth, she surely holds great and powerful magic. Magic that you can harness just by asking her, acknowledging her, and of course honoring her.

I hope that you enjoy this book as much as I enjoyed writing it. If you did, it would be wonderful if you could take a short minute and leave a review on Amazon, as your kind feedback is much appreciated and so very important.

Thank you.

REFERENCES

Andrews, R. (2018). The moon is electric, especially when it's full. *National Geographic Magazine.* https://www.nationalgeographic.com/science/article/news-full-moon-electric-ionosphere-nasa-artemis-space

Brown, R. & Gerberg, P. (2012). The healing power of the breath: Simple techniques to reduce stress and anxiety, enhance concentration, and balance your emotions. *Shambhala, Boston.* ISBN: 10-1590309022

Cajochen. C., Altanay-Ekici, S., M., Münch, Frey, S., Knoblauch, V., & Wirz-Justice, A. (2013). Evidence that the lunar cycle influences human sleep. *Current Biology (23)*15, P1485-1488. https://www.cell.com/current-biology/fulltext/S0960-9822(13)00754-9

Criger, C. (2021). Pentacle (Wiccan). *Grove Oklahoma.com.*

https://www.cityofgroveok.gov/building/page/pentacle-wiccan

Daley, J. (2019). Oysters 0pen and close their shells as the moon wanes and waxes. *Smithsonian Magazine*. https://www.smithsonianmag.com/smart-news/oysters-sync-lunar-cycle-180971230/

Dragonsong, E. (2021). The power of the Moon. *Wicca Spirituality*. https://www.wicca-spirituality.com/power-moon.html

Dual Crossroads. (2021). *The history and symbolism of the pentagram*. https://www.dualcrossroads.com/post/the-history-and-symbolism-of-the-pentagram

Fellizar, K. & Kahn, N. (2021). Astrologers explain how the moon can affect your mood. *Bustle Magazine*. https://www.bustle.com/life/6-weird-ways-the-moon-can-affect-your-mood-17020547

Gannon, M. (2013). A bewitching history: Why witches ride broomsticks. *LiveScience.com*. https://www.livescience.com/40828-why-witches-ride-broomsticks.html

Gardner, G. (1950). The Gardnerian Book of Shadows. *Forgotten Books*. ISBN 978-1605069333.

Ingenito, T. (2021). *The evolution of spears*. https://www.sutori.com/story/the-evolution-of-spears--sVeTKrpCsnoZdPUau4fca9Ru

Kahn, N. (2020). Mark your calendar for September's practical new moon. *Bustle Magazine*. https://www.bustle.com/life/next-new-moon-calendar

McDermott, N. (2019). Car crashes are more common during a full moon with men particularly vulnerable to the 'werewolf effect', research reveals. *The Sun*. https://www.thesun.co.uk/motors/9048871/car-crashes-common-during-full-moon/

OtherWorldly.com. (2019). *The witch's cauldron: Origins, magic & how to use a cauldron today*. https://otherworldlyoracle.com/witchs-cauldron/

Poppick, L. (2013). 6 Wild ways the moon affects animals. *Live Science Magazine*. https://www.livescience.com/37928-ways-the-moon-affects-animals.html

WICCA SPELL BOOK FOR BEGINNERS

*Learn Witchcraft Rituals, White,
Red, Black, and Rune Magic
with this Easy-to-Read Guide*

Frank Bawdoe

INTRODUCTION

Believe it or not, there are more than a million practicing Wiccans and pagans in the U.S. today. Wicca is a commonly misunderstood religion whose members identify themselves as "witches." It is a peaceful, spiritual and nature-based practice that has zero to do with Satanism. Nowadays, there is a growing misunderstanding that a person who identifies as being a witch is "the Wicked Witch of the West."

Frank Bawdoe is an author and devoted spiritualist who is resolved in his dedication to the philosophy of Wicca and Paganism. Frank has a deep desire to coach readers in their desire to learn about the essence of life and to teach and empower them on the basics and fundamentals of magic spells. Included in this book are the different options for crafting spells. They include multiple different types of spells, tools, materials, proper instructions, and information necessary for you to succeed with the magic spells you will practice based off of this book. Frank Bawdoe has authored numerous books on Wicca and Paganism, including *Witchcraft Religion & Spirituality and New Age Divination.* An ardent knowledge seeker who proudly walks the path leading to spirituality, he leverages his knowledge to understand the fascinating ways of life.

Exploring the depths of paganism with utmost faith and persistence for truth, Frank studies the Wiccan culture, meditation, visualization, magic, and spells to build a better connection with his inner self. Passionate about transforming lives and directing souls, Frank Bawdoe pens down his knowledge of successful spell casting and with his words, and he shines a light on the path leading to self-development, happiness, and spirituality. Frank never missed out on an opportunity to embrace the beauty of life, and surrounds himself with nature that scintillates the soul and soothes the mind. He devotes his free time to reading, writing, meditating, and exploring the mysteries of life.

Learning magic spells can actually enhance your life, help you to solve challenging problems, and improve your mental ability. With this magical guide to the powerful and best witchcraft spells, you can be the captain of your own ship steering through the tides of destiny. If you're new to spell craft, you must be familiar with the usual stereotype portrayed by Hollywood. The truth is that modern day Wiccan witchcraft is a spiritual and reliable way to express your deepest intentions and then make them come true. A spell is just a ritual where you use your energy, intentions, and inner-spiritual powers to fulfill a specific purpose you desire. Protective or white magic has never really been discouraged like destructive or Black magic, for obvious reasons.

Witchcraft Rituals/Spells

You are conducting a ritual when you cast spells because you are creating a change in the direction you want your path or your journey in life to follow. To be successful in goal attainment, it is important to symbolize your dedication, which means focusing your energy and efforts into your intentions while performing the ritual. It is also very important to display your gratefulness to a Deity or Higher Self when you end a session, thanking them for connecting with you and changing your life for the better! Hence, you must make sure to be concise about what you *really* want. That is the only way it works. If you are not absolutely sure about exactly what you want, how would you know if your spell worked, anyway? Imagine the actual images and attach them to your words. Keep a very positive frame of mind (**knowing** that you will achieve your desires), and then, we will discuss how to have your own key for unlocking the door that leads to wherever you wish. The power of the spell will give you the willpower to keep consistency in your life.

If you are just starting out, know this: many people cast spells and perform rituals every day. You do not have to be an experienced witch to create a sacred space and cast your spells at home. You just have to know a few basics, such as the importance of positive energy that raises your vibrations; the location also has to be a calm and safe personal space to practice your magic. If you want fast results, you need to have great confidence in your spell and how you cast it. Empowerment is essential to make magic happen, and you can get that from your inner strength. Whether you are female or male, learning the techniques of witchery will enable you to master your practice and fulfill your desire to become a skilled spell caster. Rituals and spells can bring opportunities into your life, but it will still be up to you whether or not to seize those opportunities and achieve your true potential. Your patience and efforts will pay off if you believe in your spell and stay focused during the session. The two essential aspects of casting successful spells are focus and belief.

CHAPTER ONE:
WITCHCRAFT RITUALS

Intention

An intention is making a decision about what you want to achieve with a spell, and then, communicating it as concisely and specifically as you possibly can. Part of the reason you are setting an intention is to clearly communicate your desires. It is important to let the deities (or the universe or higher power) know exactly what you want. Remember you are co-creating magic with a power other than yourself. Another important purpose for your intention is to not manifest the wrong outcome by mistake.

Let's say you want more money so you cast a money spell, but it is really because you hate your job. The question here is murky. Set your truths in your intention. It may not be more money that you actually want. Maybe it is life satisfaction! Maybe the spell you need to do is for finding work that you love that will also bring financial abundance.

Another purpose of your intention is where the power in the spell comes from. Once you have set your intention, you can support it with your feelings and thoughts and when put together, it will harness the power you need to make it happen. That is how to create the strongest possible intention! As you become a more powerful witch, you will see more positive changes happening in your life. New opportunities will open up for you. When you feel a deep connection to your own intuition and to the powers that be, you will start to have the confidence to take even bigger risks for bigger payoffs and make leaps and bounds towards your goals. You can get excited as a newbie witch to see for yourself that magic is real! Here is a word of caution: if a spell doesn't work the first time, don't let that stop you from trying your hand at spell casting again and again. You will soon learn there are some other factors that go into successful spellcasting.

Setting a strong and clear intention prior to beginning is the best way to power up your spell. Afterall, it is the intention of the witch that makes or breaks the spell! Here is a simple formula for the beginner or intermediate witch to try:

1. **A specific want (as precise as you can) + the time frame you want it to manifest = your intention.**

    a. Write your intention down using "I" and a verb in the present tense, as if it has already been manifested. For example: "I run two miles a week to better my health" feels stronger than "Help me to make it two miles when I run."

    b. Test your intention. Once you have written down an accurate and clear intention, conduct the following ritual(s) to test it.

        i. Journal Ritual: In a safe and calm atmosphere where you know there will be no distractions for at least ten minutes, scribe a candle and get comfortable. (You will also learn how to create a sacred space). Start journaling about how your life is at the present. Be as specific as you feel comfortable with. If you are doing a spell for love, journal your current relationship status. Write about its ups and downs. If you are looking for love, journal about what your life will feel like after you find your soulmate. What you will do together. How it feels to go for a walk on the beach with that special someone.

ii. Once you feel you have filled in all of the specifics, you can write your actual intention. For example, a good intention may be written something like this: "This month, I meet a special person who I have a spiritual, emotional, and physical connection with. We love each other passionately and openly and we are both so happy that we are going to travel together."

c. Spiritual Connection Ritual Meditation

i. Sit calmly and quietly with your eyes closed.

ii. Make a decision with whom you are communicating:

1. The Triple Goddess
2. The Great Horned God
3. The Green Man
4. Goddess Brighid

5. The horned fertility god Cernunnos
6. Isis
7. The Elements (Air, Fire, Earth, Water, Spirit)
8. Your intuition

i. Aloud, ask your spiritual guide "What is my desire?"
ii. Now listen. Pay close attention to any smells, sights, sounds, and tastes; notice your thoughts as they glide through your mind as you rest there. That could be your spirit communicating with you.
iii. If you are not receiving an answer, ask again. Ask as often as you have to until you feel you have completed your intention.

d. Visualize your Intention
   i. With your eyes closed for a specific amount of time, in your mind's eye, picture your life after your desire has been met. Focus on a specific scene; a moment in time that you believe totally represents what your life will be like after your spell. For example: If you desire a new love

interest, you can picture a scene with a new love in your mind of the two of you cuddled up on the couch, popcorn in the middle, watching *Gone with the Wind*. You will notice fairly fast if you have the right intention because you will already be viewing the results in your mind's eye, just like watching a movie! If something is not quite right, make some adjustments here and there in your scene and try again. Tweak it as much as you have to until your intention is exactly what you want.

Clearing and Cleansing Ritual

Clearing and cleansing your space and yourself is like making a blank energetic slate. Smudging is always the first line of defense to rid or ward off unwanted or negative energy. Using plants, like sage and resins to rid unwanted and negative energy, will strengthen your intention and put you in the right mindset for magic! Sage actually has antibacterial properties.

First off, making your area sacred requires clearing all of the noise and clutter so that the elements and the spirit world can hear you clearly.

1. With a vacuum and dust rag, get rid of all dirt and dust from your sacred space. If you are in your office, have an organized desk.
2. Take a ritual shower. It shows respect for the magic. Hang a bit of eucalyptus in the shower for its healing properties.
3. Feel free to adorn your workplace with crystals to enhance your spell work. Choose them according to the spell.
4. Optionally, spray any counter tops or furniture with witch hazel.
5. Run a selenite wand over your body from the bottom of your feet to the top of your head, covering all of your chakras while focusing your intention on riding the area of negativity.
6. Use sound bowls and tuning forks. They help vibrate energy right into your body and your spirit.
7. Smudge: smudging frees the spirit of protection in the plant to help you with your magic. Make sure to show great appreciation for the resin or plant you burn! If you have a bundle, simply light one end on fire and then

blow it out. Wave the smoke over all of your chakras, reaching down to the floor, up in front of you, and behind you (if you are limber enough to do so, if not, there is a healing spell for that too). If you are using loose tea or herbs, keep them in a fireproof container, light them up, and when they smoke, using a feather or your hand, wave the smoke over your body. Smudge everything you want cleansed, including your tools, altar, even the whole room. Pay special attention to doorways and corners.

8. If you can't handle smoke or you want to smudge a space where smoke is not allowed, buy a smudging spray from a trusted metaphysical store online, or make a cleaning spray.

    a. Smokeless Smudging Recipe: 1 oz. Clean spray bottle, six drops of sage essential oil, 1 tablespoon witch hazel, 1 teaspoon sea salt, spring water or water blessed by the moon, and a small clear quartz crystal that will fit into the bottle. Combine all ingredients and spray your area.

Candle Magic

In case you are wondering if you have yet to perform magic, ask yourself if you have ever made a wish before you blew out the candles on your birthday cake. Effective, easy, and quick, practicing candle magic doesn't require any experience or a religious doctrine. Candles are a great place to start your magic practice. They are easy to collect and most are inexpensive and beautiful to have around your home. There is just something so special about the glow of a candle. It is mesmerizing. Are you ready to create some wonderful candle magic? Let's start!

Step One:

Your magic wand is your words; speak your intention. Take some deep breaths to clear your mind. Ask yourself what you wish to manifest right now in your life and tell yourself that you are planting your wish into the universe like planting a seed in the soil. It is very important to understand that there is no such thing as putting a spell on someone. Instead of wishing for Michael at the gym to notice you finally, wish for your own special and beautiful mojo to be enhanced to bring you the very best love interest in your life. Using positive energy, create your intention into a condensed powerful and clear sentence.

Step Two:

Decide if your intention is big or small. For a quick lift, you can grab some of those small white candles at the local grocery store and they only take about two hours to burn down. If you're asking for something a bit bigger and want to concentrate your positive vibrations on it for a week or two, you can use a glass seven-day candle to do the trick. The size or your candle doesn't matter nearly as much as how much intention, focus, and energy you put into it. You can make a more powerful ritual candle through anointing, carving, and/or dressing it. You can dress your candle in oils and herbs, such as rose oil or olive oil. You also can blend oils to match your intentions such as money oils or love oils. To conjure up a vial of money oil start with ⅛ cup extra virgin olive oil, and then put 2 drops each of ginger and vetiver, 1 drop of orange, and 5 drops each of sandalwood and patchouli. You can find recipes for oils online.

Next, think about carving your intention into your candle. Outline any symbols or just write in words your intention starting at the top of the candle, then carve into the middle and the bottom.

Rub your hands in your anointing oil and rub down your candle as if you are manifesting your intentions into the candle starting at the top, all the way down to the bottom. However, if you are doing a banishing ritual, start rubbing your oil in the middle first, rub toward the top, then back to the middle, then to the bottom. Follow the same ritual with herbs, sprinkling them in the same patterns. Also, you can take different color candle wax and drip it on top of your oil or herbs to keep your herbs fixed on the candle. Only use a small bit of herbs; you don't want them to catch fire.

Step Three:

Magic with colors can express many different emotions which are unique to each one of us. Think about the color of your intention. A guideline is included below:

Color	Intention	Magic Tips
Red	Love, passion	Wear a sexy red scarf or article of clothing when you lit your red candle for added intent.
Orange	Confidence, creativity	Mindfully, with intention, peel and eat an orange each day from a bowl of oranges kept on your kitchen or dining table. Then lit

		your orange candle and you will have added intent.
Pink	Friendship, self-care, empathy, nurturance	Carve your name into your pink candle to show self-love before lighting it. Or carve a friend's name you mean good for.
Purple	Empowerment, royalty	Add some lavender oil or spray in the room where you are lighting the candle. Dance around your candle in the lavender scent before or after lighting.
Blue	Calm, peace, protection	Keep some seashells by your candle or in a bowl of water.
Green	Money, starting a new business, fertility	Light your candle while sitting outside, if not too windy, or wear green nail polish or a green shirt.
White	Blank slate, add sprinkles to make it the color you need. White fills in for all colors	Meditate while imagining a white orb surrounding your body after lighting your candle.

Step Four:

Write or type down your daily vision, the color of your candle. Scripting on to your candle will give your vibration an instant boost. Scripting is about writing down your calling for the day as if you have already achieved it. Write down the details, describing to yourself how it feels and what your sensations of happiness, joyousness, and freedom feel like. This will elevate your energy vibrations. Now, you are ready to carve your candle. If you do not want to burn the entire candle, carve a line however far down you want to burn to confine your spell into the top section. When it burns down to that line you can blow it out and save the rest of the candle for another spell.

Opening and Closing a Circle Ritual

"We are a circle, within a circle, with no beginning and never ending."

While facing north, speak aloud "I am grateful for your energy, precious earth; farewell." Closing or opening a circle is a technique for respecting the elements and thanking them for assisting you to take all of the energy you have built and release it. Next, while facing west, you will release the water and speak aloud "I am grateful for your energy, precious Water; I bid you adieu." Do the same with fire while facing south "Farewell Fire, thank you for your energy." End on the north, releasing the element spirit, "Spirit, I bid you goodbye for now, I close this circle, sending the energy back into the ground".

Step-by-Step Instruction on How to Cast a Circle

1. Scrub your space with burning sage, vacuum and clean it.
2. Mark the directions and elements with crystals or candles. Using a cross pattern set the south, north, east and west. Use a pentacle if you're also including the spirit.
3. Face east and name each element, moving clockwise to each point. "I call upon the element of fire." "I call upon you, Earth."
4. Meditate for a few minutes until you feel centered and grounded.
5. Connect with each element, envisioning in your mind how the wind feels blowing around you, how the water feels, etc., until you have called and connected to each element and completed your circle.
6. Now you should be facing north; imagine yourself shooting light from the bottom of your feet down into the Earth's core and pulling back its energy. State aloud "With these five elements and under the Spirit of

the Goddess, I cast protection above, below, and within this circle!"
7. You are now ready to cast your spells.

Creating your Altar

You can cast spells without being at your altar, of course, but having one is a very good place to practice and focus your intention and energy. It is a sacred space where you can communicate with the elements, goddesses, and the spirit realm in general. It doesn't have to be a special table; you can make one just about anywhere you feel drawn to. I have mine in my office, in the corner facing the west to see the sunset. I have had many altars, but a while back, I decided I wanted an altar that I could leave spell work upon without disturbance. A spell works for as long as you have it placed, in writing or words, along with all of the magical items supporting it on the altar. Every Wiccan's or pagan's journey is unique to them, so make sure you feel connected to anything that touches your altar.

Choose a cloth that you love for your altar. You can choose any pattern, color, or texture. I strongly suggest using something natural. You can even use a bamboo matt or silk; it really is up to your intuition. Here are some helpful hints for picking the color of your cloth:

Red	Fire	Love, physical energy, desire passion, will power, courage
Green	Earth	Abundance, money, fertility, nature, health, luck
Yellow	Air	Intelligence, happiness, memory
Blue	Water	Wisdom, spirituality, calmness
Orange	Fire	Buying property, intellect, justice
Pink	Fire	Friendship, nurturing, healing, romance
Brown	Earth	Nature, family, animals, gardening, cooking, grounding
White	Air	Cleansing, purity, peace, light, inspiration, clarity
Purple	Spirit	Acceptance, sexuality, balance, psychic attributes
Silver	Water	Astral projection, dreams, telepathy, intuition
Gold	Fire	Fame, fortune, wealth, luck, attention enlightenment,

If honoring a deity, include symbols or items that are attributed to them and their magic. Use your intuition when and where you are placing sacred items on your altar. Usually, five candles are placed on the altar in the four corners and in the middle. Also, you can place items representing the earth, water, fire and air. I use a glass bowl filled with purified water, small candles floating atop, and a small opal crystal at the bottom. I am exalting honor to water on the altar's west side. You can use any type of items symbolizing what you want, but here are some suggestions:

- East (Air) — Wing, feather, knife, magnifying glass, wind chimes, incense;
- West (Water) — Driftwood, seaweed, goblet, river rocks, water bowl, seashells, salt, crystal ball;
- South (Fire) — Cactus, candles, lava stones. yellow flowers, orange or red crystals, matches, spicy foods;
- North (Earth) — bones, plants, rocks, small trees, seeds, soil.

Runes Ritual

Usually inscribed in stone, the runic alphabet contains symbols that, when read, will give you answers and great insight regarding any situations or questions you may ask them. There are 24 runes, the first six of which spell the word *futhark*. The term rune means "hidden secret" or "mystery." The word *futhark* is the name of the writing system used as early as the 3rd century by Germanic people, mainly Anglo-Saxons and Scandinavians. With runes, you can use your magic to seek advice and give yourself insight into your future or someone else's. Practicing fortune-telling techniques is knowing the art of runic divination.

How to read runes:

1. Meditate in a quiet place focusing on the story you want to read. Put some deep thought into the questions.
2. Call upon the elements, goddess, or spirit of your choice to guide you.
3. Choose one rune and think about why it is significant. After some practice you can work on layouts and casts.
    a. The Three Rune Layout: randomly pick and place three runes on your sacred cloth. Place the first rune to the right, the second one in the middle, and the third one to the left. The last one is your question or the past. The middle one is the present or the present challenge. The first one rune is the answer or the future.

b. The Five Rune Layout: pick five runes and place face up or face down in the following pattern: #1-middle, #2 to its left; #3 -top: #4-bottom; #5-right place the rest in pattern of a cross encircling #1 around it. 2-5-1 horizontally symbolize your past, present and future. #4 identifies the problem or challenge you are asking or facing. and #3 gives you what you are seeking (truth--answers).
c. The Nine Rune Cast: select 9 runes and cup them in your hands for a couple of minutes while meditating on your quest. Scatter them randomly. The middle rune is the current situation or your question. The outer edges of the scatter are less relevant. Notice if the runes are touching; they may be associated. Those that have fallen opposite each other symbolize opposing forces, actions, ideas, or thoughts. Runes that fell face up are for reflection and those that are upside down are the future.

CHAPTER TWO:
WHITE MAGIC SPELLS

Casting a spell happens when you focus your intentions on your desired outcome and then stay positive about it to manifest your desired outcome. It takes a lot of practice, so be okay with losing your focus here and there. It happens to me a lot. I find meditation really helps me to not lose my focus during spell work. First, here is a simple recipe that you will probably use more than you realize. It is a moon-blessing spell.

Crystal Magic

Crystals and other mineral stones are surprisingly versatile and are powerful agents of magic. Witches and other pagans use crystals for many positive intentions, such as prosperity, love, health and wellness, and for cleansing and charging other magical tools. If you have ever looked closely at a gemstone while holding it up to the light, you can see the wonder of these special rocks and can be easily overcome with a sense of awe. The term crystal is defined as any material naturally formed by a geological process inside the Earth. Each crystal has its own special vibrational energy; the most popular is clear quartz. You will notice many of the spells in the book use crystals as a powerful vehicle for carrying your intentions and your intuition in your craft.

Many witches consider crystals to be living organisms because of the healing energies they provide. Many give off electrical charges you can see if you simply tap them with a small hammer. Spell casters understand that crystal magic is the same as magic produced by the elements as they occur naturally, like powerful storms and rushing rivers. All energies, both visible and invisible are interconnected. Since our thoughts and our intentions are also energy forms, crystals work as conduits, sending our desires and powers out into the spiritual world.

Essential Oils and Magic

Using essential oils in magic is not a new trend by any means. Ancient Egyptians used essential oils for religious ceremonies thousands of years ago. Currently, most people have experienced aromatherapy. They either love using it in their homes or when getting a massage. Essential oils affect people on many levels. Smelling an essential oil for its calming effects or to stimulate creativity are two common "everyday" ways people practice magic, whether they know it or not. Less conventionally, essential oils are used in our magic rituals. Most experienced witches are familiar with the magical properties contained in essential oils, but if you are new to the practice, know they are very powerful tools for every witch's tool kit.

Considering the fact that this is a book of spells, it is quite obvious that many ingredients or materials go into the art of magic. Ginger, sage, sugar, salt, garlic, basil, are just a few of the common ingredients. Essential oils are used to amplify the magic of these ingredients. They are used to charge crystals, in rituals, talisman, amulets, and even to anoint our physical bodies. In addition, they are also used to create powerful witchcraft goods. Candles, charms, and incense are often enhanced with a drop or two of an essential oil tailored to their intention. Essential oils are extracted from the stems, leaves, and flowers of varying types of plants. Plants carry magical energies as they are intelligent living beings. That alone makes them powerfully magical. Each plant has its own unique magical properties, and when concentrated in an oil, its magical abilities are amplified. It is important that you know to only use natural oils. Synthetic oils may smell good; however, they are not natural and are not the same as the derivatives found in botanical oils. Also, the powerful scent of an essential oil has a profound impact on the spirit, mind, and body. Hence, they are capable of altering the way the mind thinks. Just think about how you feel about your favorite scent. Does it make you happy, elevate your mood, ease your stress, or make you feel dreamy? Now, that is magic!

Types of Magical Essential Oils

1. Lemon: regarded highly for its magic in promoting clarity. Also increases your energy levels, enhances your overall wellbeing, and has rejuvenating properties.
2. Lavender: regarded highly for its relaxation and anxiety reducing properties. It is a mood stabilizer and can be used in love spells,

healing spells, sleep spells, dream recall spells, healing spells, and more.
3. Eucalyptus: is known to improve your ability to concentrate. It is also a purifying agent, dream stimulator, and can be used for many issues surrounding the nose, throat, lungs, and muscular issues.
4. Peppermint: is amazing at promoting mental clarity. It also provides protection, invites love, stimulates regeneration, and is an antiseptic used for purification and cleansing.
5. Chamomile: prized for its extreme anti-anxiety qualities and used to alleviate insomnia. This essential oil will elevate your inner peace, calm your anger, and heighten sexual arousal. It is also used for good luck and elevated spiritual awareness. Chamomile is a powerful meditation agent.
6. Clove: is used to boost energy levels, ward off the evil eye, purifying, ritual cleansing, and pain management. It has highly invigorating qualities and sparks nostalgia.
7. Frankincense: is a very ancient essential oil that provides great comfort, evokes visions, improves concentration, and is regarded highly in purification rituals.
8. Jasmine: Known as the love drawing essential oil, jasmine also attracts love on a spiritual

level, so it is the essential oil of choice for anyone searching for their soulmate.
9. Cinnamon: if you want to protect your home from all that is negative, use cinnamon essential oil in your protection spells. As it is an oil connected to the Fire Element, it is very good for stimulating the libido. It is also used in money drawing spells and will give any of your intentions a hefty boost.

Essential Herbs and Magic

Historically, there was no difference between medicine and magic. Without the rich tradition of European magic, science, and pharmacology, present-day medicines and science would never have come to be. There is a plethora of supportive documentation as to the essential role of herbal magic in the origin of present-day medicine. The only way to truly comprehend the role herbal magic plays in modern medicine is to know how it started and what it has come to be throughout the past millennium. Natural magic, as it was referred to at the start of the 1900s, was predominantly anchored in the assumption that the world was created by God in a continuous chain of life, where every element was not only linked but corresponded to another element in the unbroken chain created by God and underlying it all is purpose. Since God doesn't make any mistakes, there is a purpose for all that exists in the universe. It was understood that clues were left by the Creator or God (e.g., the flesh of a walnut in its shell and the human brain) and that magic was part of how we can affect one another. The role of the magician was to discover these correspondences and their specific magical effect and use it for the purpose of humankind.

Herbal healing, like other forms of magic, dates back to the beginning of humankind. The history of this relationship is documented by original plant medicines and herbs themselves becoming preserved historical monuments. Acknowledgment of the herbal use in pharmacology started with the pursuit of medicine through using flowers, barks, leaves, stems, seeds, and fruits of plants to remedy illness and disease. Modern day medicine has realized that the active ingredients in herbs contribute to a wide range of medicines which originate in plants. This was known to ancient civilizations and has been used throughout millennia.

Magical Herbs

1. Sage: is familiar to most witches, having been used in smudging rituals to expel negative energy left behind by repulsive furniture or even more revolting exes. For rituals, make sure to use natural sage or garden sage. White sage has become at-risk for being over-harvested so growing a bit of your own is helpful or substitute it with any form of culinary sage.
2. Rosemary: is used for many purposes. It has a stimulating scent and helps with memory. It has attributes in the areas of healing, love, protection, and feminine powers. You can hang it in your doorway, sprinkle it on the floor prior to a sweep, or in an essential oil to anoint your body.
3. Roses: are for love and friendship and so much more. Roses in the herbal world are known for calming the nervous system and unblocking and balancing the heart chakra. Fresh petals can be used for a love bath, infused into blessed water, and placed on your altar for self-care rituals.
4. Basil: is distinctly pronounced as a magical herb, making it a staple in the gardens of many a witch. It has a reputation that is

sacred, dating back to ancient cultures. It keeps you focused, brings business good luck, repels unwanted love interests, mends rifts that occur in friendships, and protects your house and your sacred circles.

5. Mint: raises the vibrations of a sacred circle, altar, and bedroom. It is used to attract positive spirits, love, to stimulate sexual arousal, attract visions, and to attract money. It has various medicinal properties as well as being a digestive aid and soothing agent for sore throats and colds. Mint is also connected to Hades because it was used to cover the scent expelled from dead bodies during funeral ceremonies in ancient Greece.

6. Mugwort: enhances psychic dreaming and divination. Its magical uses include working against fatigue, poisons, and injury. It is thought to induce astral traveling and lucid dreaming. It can be smoked, consumed as a spice, or applied to the skin. It can be used for many psychic teas and divinatory incenses.

7. Vervain: is used for protection, purification, consecrating and cleansing sacred spaces, and in ritual magic. When consumed as a tea, it helps in divination and astral projection. It is the herb of love potions and love spells.

8. Lavender: wards off evil eye and promotes peace. It is used for calming and purification. It has been documented as far back as before the time of Christ to relieve sore throats, headaches, and indigestion. Modern magic uses lavender for stress management, anxiety, digestion, fatigue, and more. It can be burned and the ashes scattered to bring harmony and peace to the home and to cleanse a sacred space. When placed under a person's pillow or consumed as a tea, its healing for ailments such depression and insomnia is unrivaled. Hanging dried lavender in front of the house will drive away evil spirits.
9. Cinnamon: is used to purify the home or sacred space of negative energy. It can be steeped into an elixir for heightened clairvoyance and psychic abilities. It is used to draw money and is great to keep in a mojo bag for inspiration. Hang a bundle over your front door to protect against outsiders with bad intentions; or make it part of your love spells. Bake a custard or cake for blessings of everlasting love and serve it in a meal if you want some luck for the night. Put it in your bag of runes for added clairvoyant energy.

Frank's "Moon-Blessed Water" Recipe

Ingredients:

- 1 Moonstone or clear quartz crystal
- A full moon
- 1 Stick cinnamon
- 1 lavender colored flower
- Glass jar or bottle with cork
- Cauldron or cast-iron pot for boiling
- Cheesecloth, coffee filter, or strainer
- Funnel
- 1 White floating candle

What to do:

1. Find out when the next full moon occurs, you're going to need it.
2. Gather all of your ingredients on the full moon night. If you are feeling super witchy, do this spell with a traditional pot on the flames of your bonfire! Or just use a stovetop burner.
3. Bring the herbs and water to a boil. If you put them in a cheesecloth or wrap and tie them in a coffee filter, you won't have to strain the liquid later.
4. Let the whole kit and kaboodle simmer on a low heat for 30 minutes.

5. After it cools, strain the herbs into the glass bowl.
6. At midnight, go with your bowl outside and put it where you can see the moon's reflection in the water.
7. Place your clear quartz or moonstone crystal in the middle of the bowl.
8. Light your candle and send it floating in your moonlit water. You can either meditate until it burns out or ask the Goddesses to compliment the moon with her blessings. Leave it there until the next day.
9. The next day, pick out the cold wax from the candle encasement.
10. Pour the water through the funnel.
11. Thank all spirits involved and your materials.
12. Keep it handy!

Frank's Healing Spell to Keep you Safe and Sound (Basic Healing Spell)

Materials

- Candles

- 1 White for cleansing, peace, and purity
- 1 Pink for close friendships
- 1 Green for health and prosperity
- 1 Purple for spiritual strength
- Crystal: 1 Clear Quartz (master healer)
- Pen and paper to scribe your name or another person or a photo of yourself or the person you want to heal. Do this spell for one person at a time for the most strength.
- Healing oils:
  - Lavender is a natural antidepressant, decongestant, good for skin problems, and is a natural diuretic.
  - Chamomile is a natural antidepressant, antibiotic, lessens acne, anti-inflammatory and helps with insomnia. Sparks sweet dreams.
  - Eucalyptus calls on the spirit of the koala bear. Promotes positivity and healing energy.
  - Cinnamon oil boosts your spell's power and aids in healing and balancing chakras.
- Large plate
- Fire in the form of a lighter

Steps

1. Decide where you are going to cast your spell and cleanse your sacred area and yourself.
2. Sit down in a quiet spot with all of your ingredients in front of you.
3. Write your name or the name of the person you want to heal on a piece of paper or use a photo and put it into your fireproof container, cauldron, plate, etc.
4. Cup the clear quartz crystal in your hands to warm it up. Focus on the crystal, imagining you are filling it with love and healing energy, and then, place your crystal on top of the name or photo.
5. Fix the candle by placing one drop of each oil on each candle (anointment ritual).
6. Anoint each of your candles with a drop of each oil. All of the oils in this spell are for healing. You can use your intuition on which oil goes on each candle.
7. Place the candles in a circle around the container with the name or photo. They should be evenly spaced in the four cardinal points.
8. Using the lighter or a match, light your candles.
9. Gaze into the flames and picture a fire circling around the name or photo of yourself or the

person you want to heal. Imagine the fire turning the dark to light, the suffering to healing.

10. With your eyes closed, imagine the healing glow flowing into the person through the crystal. Know they are healthy and well, vital, and glowing with energy and wellness. Speak aloud as if the healing has already taken place. "I am happy and healthy and healed. My heart is strong and healthy."

11. Picture a smile on the face of the person looking back at you with love and strength. If you are casting the spell on you, imagine how happy you are to be feeling better, how your arms and legs feel light, and how endlessly capable you are of magic.

12. Now direct your power to the specific ailment. Imagine flooding that area with healing light; the longer and more focused you are the more powerful the spell.

13. When you feel your spell is complete. Slowly open your eyes and speak aloud

With all of the magic in this spell, I cast healing energy, protection, and light to (the name of the person). I send this magic and vigor flowing through my/their being so it

may heal them of their suffering. So Mote it Be.

"Peaceful Mind" Spell (for Calming)

- 1 Blue candle
- 1 Purple Candle
- 1 White Candle
- A palo santo stick and fireproof dish
- White paper and a blue pen

Steps

1. Put the candles in a triangle.
2. White at the top point, blue to the right, and purple to the left.
3. Light them in this order: Blue, Purple, White.
4. Light the palo santo.
5. Speak this spell three times.

   I have the courage to break free and the insight to know. With the breath of this sacred smoke, calmness will grow. So Mote it be.

6. Take ten deep breaths through your nose and out of your mouth.
7. Smudge the pen and paper with your palo santo bundle.

8. Trust in your intuition and write your intention on the paper.
9. Read what you have written and meditate on it for five minutes.
10. Keep the paper with you for as long as you need it.

Bathing Spells for Spiritual Cleansing and Protection

Spiritual bathing offers added protection, especially if you are feeling vulnerable. The following spells are ideal for strengthening your spiritual protection barriers. Spiritual bathing practices are utilized in many cultures for clearing the mind, cleansing the soul, and healing your chakras. Make sure your tub or shower is free of clutter and spotless. The ingredients mentioned below, meditation, and most of all intention, are elements for successful magic. Also, please be sure to be unplugged (no cell phone or other devices). It is time for you to meditate and focus on invoking the spirit of elements and deities for healing, protection, prosperity, and love. These spells can also be used with the intent of cleaning away negativity or unwanted situations that may be holding you back. There is no set way to take a spiritual bath. Each bath is prepared and set to each individual's needs, but if you find yourself needing assistance, below you will find some steps that others have taken to create a great spiritual bath experience.

Materials (these can be added or switched with any of the ingredients listed for bathing spells).

- Salt (The most powerful salt is black)
- Dead sea salt
- Kosher salt
- Eucalyptus oil
- Cedar oil
- Four small blue candles
- Mint leaves
- Rosemary
- Lavender

Steps

1. Protective Bath Spells
    a. Protective bathing spell 1. Charge your kosher salt: "I summon the spirit of the salt to help me to protect my home and heart." Mix 5 drops of eucalyptus oil and 5 drops cedar oil with ½ cup of kosher salt with bath water.
    b. Protective bathing spell 2. Basil, rosemary, lavender, mint, handful of sea salt. Run a warm bath and toss in ingredients. Save a cup of the water after bathing and toss it outside.

c. Protective bathing spell 3. Ingredients: 1 bay leaf, 1 teaspoon ground mint leaf, 1 teaspoon fresh or ground rosemary, ¼ cup coarse salt, 1 small white candle and a pot or tea kettle. If using fresh herbs, you can double the amount.

   i. Add herbs to a pot of spring water and bring to a boil. Let simmer for 15 minutes.
   ii. While the tea is cooking, take a normal shower to physically clean yourself.
   iii. Light your candle and fill your tub with warm water.
   iv. When your tea is ready, remove herbs with a filter.
   v. Starting with your head, scoop a cup of water out of the pot and pour over your spiritual bath. Work your way down to your feet.
   vi. While you are letting the spirit of the water flow over your body, Notice the smell, and thank Mother Earth for creating it.
   vii. Clear your mind during this calming time you have created for yourself.

viii. Step out and pat yourself or let yourself air dry.

"Much-Needed Sleep" Spell

We now have a good understanding about intention being at the heart of magical practice. I can't think of a more intense intention than for someone to sleep. It is very important to combine self-care with most spells, but especially this one. Learning some deep breathing techniques, watching your caffeine intake, practicing relaxation techniques, and ritual bathing can fight insomnia. After doing all these, a bit of magic at bedtime should seal the deal. After participating in the preparation for bed techniques just outlined, you will be ready to cast the Much-Needed Sleep Spell. Smoky quartz is a powerful grounding stone and prevents nightmares and clear quartz amplifies the powers of all other crystals.

Materials

- 8 Dried lavender stems
- 1 Clear Quartz Crystal
- 1 Piece of preferably raw paper (unbleached)
- 1 Smoky Quartz Crystal

Steps

1. After you perform your ritual bathing preparation for your Much Need Sleep spell, get your bedtime area to be as comfortable as possible. Dim the lights, light a nighttime candle, use fresh bed clothes (never underestimate how freshly cleaned sheets can affect the quality and quantity of sleep), take a before bedtime trip to the restroom, making sure all of the doors are locked, the pets tended to, I think you get the point. Simply put, get ready for bed.
2. Sit comfortably in your bed. Don't sit on the pillow you use for your head. If you need an extra pillow, grab one from the couch or spare bedroom.
3. Have all of your materials within reach.
4. Hold a crystal in each hand and sync your intention with each of the crystal's energies. Notice how they feel in your hand.
5. Close your eyes and roll the crystals around in your hand, feeling every bump, curve, and shape as they slowly start to warm up with your touch.
6. Let the vibrational energies of each stone enter through your fingers, spread through your arms and down your shoulders, like a gentle wave washing over your whole body.

7. Focus on the smoky quartz crystal and realize its grounding and calming powers transforming all things negative or stressful into peace and serenity as you move its energy though your legs and down to your toes.
8. Now focus on your clear quartz and realize that suddenly hope and good thoughts are beginning to radiate from the palm of your hand.
9. Feel the energy of the magnificent clear quartz flowing through your mind, body, and soul.
10. Slip into the protective and calming energy powers of the stones while allowing your mind to quiet.
11. After a few moments with the crystals, softly speak:

   Peaceful rest come visit me.
   My mind with my spirit will be free.
   Grant me contentment of mind tonight,
   so my morning will be a beautiful sight.
   So mote it be.

12. Slowly open your eyes, while staying relaxed and continuing to let the calming effects of your ritual course through your body.

13. Take the rest of the ingredients (lavender sprigs and crystals) and fold them up in the piece paper like a small parcel and place them next to your bed.
14. Gently ease yourself down into your bed.
15. Thank your crystals, your lavender sprigs, and any elements or deities that accompanied you during your spell and let yourself drift off.

Black Salt Recipe

Black salt or Witch's salt is used for many purposes. If you do use it for a voodoo or hexing make sure you dispose of it by burying it far from your home. Otherwise, sprinkle around the perimeter of your property, car, or anything else you want protected. It is an excellent way to cleanse and charge your crystals. You can use it to drive away bad spirits and you can sprinkle it on the footprints of anyone toxic in your life that needs to be somewhere else, anywhere else, except with you!

Ingredients

- 2 parts sea salt
- Ash from your fire pit or black pepper

- Food-grade activated charcoal (you can use dry, powdered black food coloring but it is not as useful as ash and charcoal.)
- Grind it up with a mortar and pestle.
- Store it in a spell bowl with a small spoon that you have smudged.

"Protect Your Home" Spell

Steps

1. Using black salt, create a circle around you.
2. Place your 4 blue candles inside of the circle in the cardinal points.
3. Light the candles.
4. Chant:

   "Salt of Earth Guard my home. Place it in a protective zone. Protect it from all that's dark. Hold it safely in your heart."

5. Focus your intention as you watch in wonderment at how the flames dance for protection.
6. When you feel the spell is complete, blow out the candles.
7. Thank the spirits with your deepest gratitude for protecting your home.

Home Protection Crystal Enchantment Spell

Materials

- One small bowl
- 1 black candle
- 1 Rose quartz
- 1 Fluorite
- 1 Clear quartz
- 1 bulb of garlic
- 3 iron nails (large)
- 9-inch-long pieces of white thread (#9)
- 9-inch-long pieces of black and red thread (#6 of each)
- Water
- Wine
- 1 White Egg

Steps

1. Take 3 white pieces of thread, 2 red pieces of thread, and 2 black pieces of thread and braid them together.
2. Light the black candle
3. Let some of the wax puddle at the top of the candle and then coat the braided thread with it. This will form a magically charged wick.

4. Do the same in the same order with the rest of your thread (twice) so that you end up with 3 braided wicks.
5. Peel some of the garlic skin and enwrap one of the iron nails.
6. Wrap one of the wicks around the nail encased in garlic skin.
7. Do the same with the other two nails and two braids, so you end up with 3 braided wicks.
8. Place the 3 nails in the bowl in the shape of a triangle.
9. In the center of the triangle, place the egg.
10. Place the crystals at each point of the triangle.
11. Sprinkle it with the wine and the water.
12. Do this for 3 days.
13. On day 4, throw the egg out into your yard, bury the crystals, and drive the nails into the ground
14. So mote be

This is a very strong spell from *The Gardnerian Book of Shadows* and should protect your house indefinitely.

"Children Need Protection" Spell

All children including witches need protection. As adults, it is our number one priority. Their spiritual, emotional, and physical health needs to be guarded against any foul doings. This is sympathetic magic to protect a child or children whom you care for.

Materials
- 2 Small Rose Quartz Crystals
- Echinacea
- Elderberry
- White cotton
- Bright yellow cloth approximately 1 ft
- Fingernail or toenail clippings from the child
- A lock of the child's hair or children's hair
- If possible, a baby tooth
- Pen and yellow paper
- Rose essential oil
- Aquamarine Crystal
- 2 Cups of Caraway Seeds
- Yellow thread
- Super glue

Steps

1. Lay your yellow cloth our and hand draw a bear or doll (see diagram below)

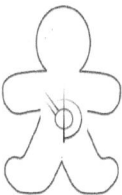

2. You can draw the protection sigil on the front. It is your puppet to put your intention into.
3. Cut two identical pieces.
4. Write the name of the child or children on the piece of paper.
5. Put two drops of rose essential oil on the Aquamarine crystal.
6. Using the yellow thread, sew the back to the front but leave the top open so you can stuff it later.
7. Write the child's name on the piece of paper and fold it up.
8. Put all of the child's personal items into the doll.
9. Put ½ of the seeds in the doll.
10. ½ way to the top put the child's name folded in the middle.
11. Put the other ½ caraway seeds.

12. Stuff the rest up into the top and wherever else needs it
13. Sew the top of the doll.
14. Super glue the blue crystals for eyes. If you don't want to use superglue, put the stones inside the doll and then sew it closed.
15. Place your doll on your altar for three days; three times a day wave your hand or wand over it with your intention spoken aloud.
16. Put the doll in a hidden spot somewhere in the child's room but out of reach. Up in a closet is one place that will protect the child. Chant:

I hide you in (child's name) room;
Protect this child with great health;
I cast the spell with tremendous stealth
For all of the love nature can throw.
Bless this child from head to toe.
So mote it be.

You can substitute the child's name for this child.

Prosperity Spells

Money spells work best when cast during a full moon. It is always smart to do your cleansing rituals and make sure to have clear intentions when you are doing magic to attract prosperity.

"Money Grows on Trees" Spell

Materials

- String
- Green cloth
- 9 Coins
- Green candle
- Ground cinnamon
- Essential oil for prosperity sandalwood or ginger

Steps

1. Do some deep breathing and then place all of the above ingredients on your cleansed altar.
2. Spend however long it takes to make sure you have positive vibes for the ritual.
3. Anoint your green candle with the prosperity oil (follow the candle dressing process from Chapter One).
4. Put your candle in its holder or on a fireproof dish and place it on your altar.
5. Place the nine coins in a circle around the candle. While you are designing the circle

with your coins, imagine you have already received the money, projecting your thankfulness.
6. Light the candle and speak the following money spell three times:

One coin here, nine coins there,
I feel my wealth everywhere.
I invite prosperity and monetary gain.
I have no more financial pain.
So mote it be.

"Money Over the Moon" Spell

This spell must be cast under a full moon. If you have a real silver coin, great; if not any silver-colored coin works just fine. Also, have on hand a silver or green cloth.

Steps

1. Position yourself under the moonlight
2. Place your coin on your cloth so that you can see the moonlight shining on it.
3. Gently wave your hands over the coin while imagining that you are gathering all of the silver in the moon.
4. Chant aloud:

Beautiful spirit of the Moon

Bring me prosperity soon.
Fill my till with all the gold.
As much as you have my hands can hold.
So mote it be.

"Witch's Bottle" Spell to Sell

Everything that goes into your witch's bottle is symbolic and all of it will attract customers to your product or service. This spell can only be performed during the new moon.

Materials

- Your business card x 2
- Clear tape
- 1 Pen
- Green ribbon
- Chocolate coins (the ones in the gold foil) or you can use real coins.
- 1 Bottle
- Honey

Steps

1. Draw a bumble bee on the back of your business card (bees are a symbol of prosperity; see diagram below).
2. On the back of the other business card, draw the sigil for good sales (see diagram below).

3. Roll the card up like a bill, put a green ribbon around it, and stick it in the bottle.
4. Add the chocolate coins (a symbol for the sale coming to you in a "sweet" fashion.) If you use real coins, cleanse them in the dirt overnight first.
5. Tape the card with the sigil for good sales across the front of the bottle.
6. Bury the bottle on the next full moon and draw a pentagram on top of the soil with the top point facing west. Leave the bottle undisturbed.

Garden Growth Elemental Spell

You can ask any witch and they will tell you that their garden is one of life's most magical places. There are many books out there devoted only to magic and gardens. Witches whose spiritual journeys are earth-based start planning their gardens in the early months of spring. The very act of starting a new life from a seed is ritualistic magic at its best, let alone the magic of watching it go from seed to seedling to sprout and then blossom. This is literally watching magic unfold right in front of our very eyes. There are lunar gardens, magical herb gardens, goddess gardens, and more. This spell is for raising an elemental garden. Midsummer or Litha is a wonderful time to start digging your garden! The earth is warm and the sun is at its peak. What you are going to do here is connect specific sections of your garden with the four elements.

Steps

1. Keeping in mind this garden is going to be circular, consider the amount of space you have and drive a ceremonial stake into the ground right in the center.
2. Tie a piece of string to the top of the stake and begin marking your perimeter by walking around in a circle.
3. Mark your circle by sprinkling black soil or birdseed.
4. Now that your circle perimeter is marked, till or dig up the soil.
5. Standing in your soon to be elemental garden, face north.
6. Divide your circle into elemental sections, so that ¼ of the circle is devoted to the directions which coincide with the elements.

7. Take some rocks or stones of your liking and mark your sections.
8. Very carefully, start to choose your plants.
   a. North is connected to the earth, which is associated with security and stability. Use honeysuckle and magnolia.
   b. East is connected to air, which is associated with mental clarity and wisdom. Use plants in the mint family, such as sage and mugwort
   c. South is connected to fire, which is associated with compassion and creativity. Plant basil and rosemary.
   d. West is connected to water, which is associated with intuition and emotion. Plant chamomile and hyssop.
9. As you begin making holes for each plant, add blessings. Dig your hands into the soil feeling it and thanking it. You can create your own little song or chant. Plants love music. You can also give an offering to each section, such as fire for the south, water for the west, and so on. This is a sacred space, so smudging is entirely appropriate.
10. Add any spiritual accessories, statues, and keep in theme with each element. Cockleshells

go well with water. They make any garden look magical.

"Rain Dance" Spell

1. Cast a sacred circle outside in the afternoon around 4:00 pm.
2. Place a clear quartz crystal at the bottom of a glass or crystal bowl and fill with spring water.
3. Program the water and the crystal with your intention; specifically mentioning rain.
4. Cup some water in your hands and dance around your circle while spilling the water from your hands 5 times chanting or singing:

   Rain, Rain, come today!
   With drops of water, come our way,
   From the sky and over the land,
   For you comes this water from my hands.
   So mote it be.

"Rain, Rain Go Away" Storm Protection Spell

Materials
- Goblet
- Wine

- White Candle
- Amber or Evergreen Incense
- Wooden spoon
- Collected, stored, and blessed rainwater (you can use your moon water, but it is good to have some protection water made from the rain).
    - If you can leave a container out during a thunderstorm the rainwater will be charged from lightning, which makes for powerful magic water.
    - If you do not have any collected rainwater, use consecrated water.

Blessed Water Instructions:

- Pour some spring water into a bowl.
- Pour some salt into the water and stir it with your hand three times in a clockwise direction.
- Wave your hands over the water and chant

    I exorcise all negativity from this creature of water, both unseen and seen, and bless thee water in the name of the divine Goddess Amphitrite.

Steps

1. Cast a sacred circle outside.

2. Light the candle and the incense.
3. Fill the goblet with a mixture of the blessed water and wine.
4. Starting at the East end of your property, take the wooden spoon and sprinkle the water along the perimeter of your property, around your car, and anywhere else you need protection from a storm. Sprinkle with the spoon. Chant:

Stormy weather, here is my offering.
Reap not your fury upon this property,
Nor my family, nor their possessions.
So mote it be.

5. Continue until you have come full circle.
6. Save a few drops of your potion for your altar and pour the rest out in the direction that the storm is coming from.

"Confidence in Me" Tea

How many times in your life have you passed up an opportunity because you were so sure you either didn't deserve it or there was no chance you would be able to achieve it? Have you passed up chances to invest in your own small business or travel on a whim? Are there times you wish you had spoken up, but were too afraid of other people's reactions?

After today, you can leave your insecurities and doubts behind and change your attitude radically. Going forward you will be confident enough to be the captain of your own ship of life thanks to a bit of magic, a few powerful crystals, and willingness of intent.

Ingredients

- Earth: Ginger root, lemon, rhodiola (boosts dopamine) or cinnamon.
- Water: The essence of your medium and the canvas carrying your magic.
- Air: The fragrances and steam arising from your potion.
- Fire: Your tea's warmth, giving you confidence.
- Spirit: All of the Elements combined in your ritual finalized with sipping your tea.

Steps

1. Keep in mind, one cup of tea will require at least one teaspoon (3 grams) of dried herbs. So, if you are making one cup of tea for 7 days in a row, you will need to blend at least 21 grams of herbs.
2. Spell out your recipe in your own handwriting. Create a name for your magical

blend and pen down your intention. Feel free to add your own incantation.
3. Blend your herbs together, while speaking your intention three times, raising the volume each time. Do it three more times, while making your voice softer each time until you have it internalized.

Goal Accomplishment Jar Spell

Materials

- Jar
- Cinnamon
- Basil
- Sage
- Rose oil
- Rosemary
- Rose quartz
- Pen and paper
- Bee drawing (see diagram in "Witch's Bottle Spell" to Sell)
- 1 Green candle

Steps

1. Light the green candle.
2. Rub some rose oil around the rim of the jar.

3. Start with a layer of sage clippings at the bottom of your jar.
4. Add a layer of cinnamon.
5. Add a layer of basil.
6. Write your goals or a goal on your piece of paper.
7. Put your rose quartz in the center of the paper and fold it up.
8. Put the parcel in the jar.
9. Cover the paper with a layer of rosemary.
10. Put your bee drawing on top of the rosemary.
11. Put the top on and place the jar where you can regularly reflect upon it.
12. Blow out the candle to activate the spell.

"Communication is a Two-Way Street" Spell

Do you wish you knew how to communicate better with your significant other(s); that you knew how to say what you mean before you say something that can cause a disconnect between you? Do you suddenly find yourself in the middle of an argument without knowing how you got there? Are you having difficulty explaining yourself or expressing your feelings? Good communication requires mutual respect and effective listening. I created this spell to help ease communication efforts, but you have to be willing to listen to your loved one without preparing a rebuttal while they are talking. If you are thinking about what you are going to say when the other person is talking, it is impossible to hear them. Remain calm, cast this spell, and then listen.

Materials

- 3 Blue candles
- Lavender incense
- Amber oil
- Cell phone
- Dill
- Oregano
- Caraway

Steps

1. This spell should be cast at your altar if it is big enough, if not, the kitchen table will do just fine.
2. Light your lavender incense and put it in your abalone shell or a fireproof dish.
3. Light your blue candle.
4. Place your cell phone in the center of your altar or table.

5. Scatter the herbs and lavender buds in a circle around your cell phone.
6. You will need three candles, one for each day. Let them burn all the way down.
7. In a clockwise motion rub the amber oil on your throat and speak the spell three times and for three days.

Communication needs trust.
Talking, we must.
I'll speak to you.
You'll speak to me.
Communication with trust will be.
So mote it be.

"New Love Spell" for Blessing a Relationship

The tingle of a new relationship can also cause angst. You may be worrying that things may go wrong. Whenever you cast a spell involving relationships, always seek permission from the other person. Otherwise, the magic can be considered a manipulation and backfire. For this spell you will have to put your kitchen witchery to the test.

1. Bake a loaf of bread.
2. In the moonlight, hold the loaf of bread up at the moon.

3. Ask Lady Diana, the Lunar Goddess to bless the bread and the new relationship.
4. While enjoying the moon with your new lover, tear a piece of the bread (do not cut it with a knife) and share it with them.

"Mend a Broken Heart" Spell

Throughout life, we experience a wide range of emotions and energies. One of the more painful experiences that can linger is a breakup. Taking the time to symbolize the meaning of these feelings through rituals allows us the ability to move past the pain and recover by moving and releasing negative or painful energies. Visualizing and imagination is a powerful tool that helps us to create our own reality. Consciously using our words or casting a spell can create more peace by speeding up the process. This is an in-depth spell for deep healing after a breakup.

Materials

- 1 white egg
- Lemon balm tea
- Essential rose oil
- 1 pink rose
- 1 pink candle
- Honey

Steps

1. Sit down in a quiet place where you will not have distractions.
2. Cup the egg in your hand.
3. Meditate on the ended relationship, paying close attention to your grief, frustration, loneliness, or other negative feelings, letting them come to the surface.
4. Do not fight the feelings; cry without fear or shame.
5. During this part of the ritual, gently roll the egg over your face.
6. Visualize the egg soaking up all of your unhappiness as if it were a sponge.
7. Once you feel the egg has soaked up all of your negative and painful emotions, take it as far away from your home as possible and bury it.
8. All of the unhappiness and depression projected into the egg will be neutralized when absorbed by the earth.
9. Return home and make some herbal tea with lemon and put in it a couple of rose petals and some honey.
10. Sit with your pink candle and place the rest of the rose petals in a circle around it.
11. As you are lighting the candle, imagine the rose petal scent connecting to the warmth of

the candle filling you and the room with loving, beautiful, and warm lights with the sweet smell of rose.

12. Using some essential rose oil, anoint your heart chakra.
13. While sipping the tea, speak aloud:

    Gentle tea with your healing art, warm my soul and soothe my heart. So Mote it be.

14. Visualize yourself surrounded and filled with peacefulness and love.
15. Know you deserve happiness and love and experience the weightlessness of being free from the past relationship.
16. Look into the flame of the candle and see your new life full of joy and happiness, fulfilled and healed; freed from the bondage of a bad relationship.

Aphrodite Beauty Oil

Ingredients

- 1 Ounce glass amber colored bottle with dropper
- 1 Tiny rose quartz crystal
- Jojoba oil as the base
- Almond oil ⅛ oz

- Vitamin E liquid ¼ oz
- Essential oils:
  - Jasmine 15 drops
  - Rose ⅛ oz
  - Ylang ylang 20 drops

Steps

1. Cleanse your rose quartz by rolling it in salt a couple of times (the salt will charge it too).
2. Fill the bottle ¼ of the way with Jojoba oil.
3. Add liquid vitamin E.
4. Add almond oil.
5. Drop the crystal into the container.
6. Add essential oils.
7. Use daily,

Black Obsidian and Clear Quartz Protection Stone Duo

Black obsidian crystals are powerful protection stones, and when amplified with a clear quartz crystal, they are even more powerful. Black obsidian obviously doesn't hide from dark energy. Instead it brings light to the darkness, strips negativity from your path, and directs you toward love. Black obsidian also has great healing properties, especially in times of personal loss. Clear quartz is the most powerful protection stone as it unblocks all of the chakras and amplifies the magic of other crystals.

Materials

- Clear quartz
- Black obsidian
- Sage plant

Steps

1. Bury both crystals in the soil of the sage plant for seven days.
2. Carry them both in your pocket for seven days.
3. Recharge them with either sage soil or by smudging as needed. You can use your intuition as a warning when your crystals start to carry negative weight. It is then time to cleanse and recharge them.

Protection Jar Spell

If you are a new witch or an experienced witch, at some point in your magical practice you should or already have come across a bottle loaded up with some very nice-looking things, such as blossoms, crystals, herbs, and salts, as well as some unusual looking items. such as spices, rusty nails, and olive oil. Maybe the jar had a top fixed by candle wax or a common artisan top. If you haven't come across a Mojo Jar, it is time to stop missing out on its intense powers. This particular Jar is mojo for protection. I love to look at it sitting on my altar and it makes a great conversation starter when people visit. This is a spell jar full of expectations and vitality that protects you from negativity. Here is how to make it.

Materials

- Pen and paper
- White candle
- Salt
- Jasmine
- White sage
- Chamomile
- Rosemary
- Rose petals

Steps

1. Everything you put into your Mojo Protection Jar should be placed in deliberately and carefully, totally expecting to oblige it. The reason for its existence is to put a bountiful source of security and wellbeing in your home or sacred space.

2. You can get your materials either from your garden or the grocery store.
3. Write your intention on your piece of paper finishing with "So Mote it Be."
4. Start layering your items according to your intuition with the message in the very middle so it is protected all around.
5. When your jar is full, light your candle and let some of the wax drip onto the jar's lid.
6. Let the candle completely burn down.
7. Recharge your jar every full moon by sitting it out under the full moon's reflection
8. Keep it where you can marvel at it but be careful not to place it where children can access it. The crystals can be a choking hazard and some jars or bottles you decide to create may have ingredients not fit for human consumption.

Banish the Dark Spells

Banishing spells are common techniques that should be cultivated by all witches. Whether banishing negativity, an unwanted spirit, an addiction, or a bad relationship, banishing provides you with the magic to clear and rid a circumstance you no longer want to have in your life and provides you with more control of what you do want in your life. The reason banishing is a foundational practice is because magic and life in general are full of uncertainties, so it is very important to learn how to protect yourself. It is an uncomfortable feeling for anyone to find themselves in a dark circumstance that they don't know how to escape; and in the world of magic, it's even worse. You really do not want to end up on the downside of another spirit or witch. The good news is you never have to be in that position. Learning how to defend yourself with magic and making your security a top priority goes a long way in providing you with the conviction you need to deal head on with any situation that arises. It is best to use banishing spells when you are in a calm and relaxed state of mind. If you're angry, your spell work can become hex-like, rather than banishing or merely ridding your life of the problem. Wiccans are very serious about never causing unintentional harm to anyone, as opposed to just having them removed from your life.

Banish by Burning

Materials

- A pen
- 1 piece of paper
- Fireproof plate or bowl
- Work surface that is heat tolerable
- Matches

This is a simple yet effective spell to execute. Start out by penning your intention, namely whatever you are intending to banish (a personal character defect such as procrastination or negative self-dialog, the name of someone or some spirit, etc.). It may be obvious, but safety first when working with smoke and fire.

1. Spend five or ten minutes focusing on what is written on your piece of paper, call out your intention as precisely as you can to whichever spiritual guide you feel faith in for this specific spell.
2. Simply, light your piece of paper on fire and drop it onto your plate.

3. While it is burning, imagine your selected target vanishing from your life and then zero in all of your imagination on how your life is like without it, as if it has already happened.
4. Once the paper is finished burning, gather the ashes and throw them outside of your house. Toss them to the wind or put them in the outside trash but do it right away.

Banish by Candle

Materials

- 1 candle holder with 1 **black** candle
- Anointing oil of your preference
- Matches
- Paper
- Salt
- Cayenne pepper
- Scribing or carving tool

Steps

1. Slowly scatter your salt in a circle, moving counterclockwise around you and your workspace, while imagining a salt barrier for your protection while casting your spell.
2. Call out your intention and scribe it into your candle. For instance you may carve "My fear is

gone" or "Larry is out of my life." You may also want to carve a banishing symbol (sigil) into your candle.
3. When you have concluded your carving, conduct your anointment with whichever oil you feel is right for the spell.
4. Sprinkle cayenne pepper over your candle.
5. Light your candle while reciting your intention aloud into a chant or mantra while your candle is burning.
6. Let the candle burn all the way down. Make sure it is sitting safely on a fireproof surface and that your pets don't singe a whisker, too.

"There's the Door" Spell for Banishing a Toxic Person from Your Life

Materials:

- Scissors
- 2 black candles
- Cayenne pepper
- 1 piece of paper or photo of the person you wish to banish.

Cast when the moon is waning for best results.

Steps

1. Light both candles.
2. Write the person's name on a piece of paper and find a photo of that person (try to get a photo, it makes the spell very strong).
3. Place the photo and the name between the two black candles.
4. Sprinkle cayenne over the flames
5. Speak the following spell,

May "name of the person" be kept away from me.
Now be gone so I can be free.
From this place "name" will depart, forever we will be apart.
This is my spell and it is strong.
My life is good now that "name" is gone.
So Mote it be.

6. Cut the photo and the paper in half and toss into the flame.

"Sacred Cleansing Water" Recipe

Steps

1. Get a large clean glass bowl and fill it ¾ of the way full.
2. Sprinkle sea salt into the water, use your intuition as to the amount.
3. Put a clear quartz in the water.

4. Place the bowl under a full or waxing moonlight overnight.
5. Pour the water into a glass bottle that you have smudged and anointed with either sweet orange, patchouli, or cinnamon essential oil.

"Removing Evil from an Object" Spell

Without a doubt, every object in your home or office holds the energy that was placed in it by you or someone else. Sometimes, we either purchase or are gifted an object that has energy embedded within it. In general, the energy is good or neutral, but what if it is bad or negative energy? There are times when we have those items in our possession and something bad has happened. You don't want to have to get rid of those objects, but they can be awful reminders of something bad. Other times, there is some ominous feeling about a random object you own. No one wants ominous energy in home or at their workplace. Well, here is what you do:

Steps

1. The object must be smudged or cleansed or the bad, negative, or even evil energy can permeate your home or office, which is the last thing you need.

2. Call upon the elements and deities to grant positive attributes, vibrations, or energies to the object you have cleansed and now need to bless.
3. It always comes down to you to set a positive intention for the object. Without a purpose, you can't assume a blessing spell will work.
4. Imagine the object glowing in a white light.
5. Bless your object with positive vibrations. Chant:

Goddesses and God of this object,
I ask you to bless this item and give it the power to make good between us.
Protect it from darkness while I sleep.
So Mote it be.

Banishing Sigil

A sigil is a symbolic representation of your intention that you create to change your circumstances and manifest your desires. Sigils seem simple but are extremely powerful.

**I AM PROTECTED FROM
NEGATIVE ENERGY**

Steps

1. To banish bad spirits from your home, bad thoughts from your head, and lust from your mind you can use banishing sigils. You can practice drawing these sigils above, if you are just starting out. Remember, everything in spellcasting is about intention and intuition, so learning how to develop yours will define the strength of your spells.
2. Cut out the sigil you have drawn and hold it your hands while visualizing your mind, home, or heart filling up with its energy and gleaming light around the exterior of your doors (if you are banishing negativity from your home) or glowing brightly around an object (if you are banishing evil from an item).
3. When you are finished with your banishing spell, burn it in an abalone shell or fold it up and put it behind a mirror.

"Walk Away your Troubles" Spell

This simple and effective spell makes perfect sense!

Materials

- 1 piece of chalk, chosen by your own decision
- Your walking shoes

Steps

1. Using the piece of chalk, write what you wish to banish on the bottom of your shoes or sneakers.
2. Go for a stroll or wear them throughout the day and with every step you take imagine your problem disappearing at the same time as the chalk disappears.

Ancestral Communion Spell

Everyone wants to communicate with their ancestors, every now and then. Sometimes, it is for comfort and sometimes for advice. Worshiping our ancestors is a very common form of religious and spiritual practice across the globe. As witches, we use meditation and rituals to get our ancestors to come to the table and lend us some of their insight. How we sense their presence is by our intuition. Their wisdom on death and life is a very valuable resource for any Wiccan. This spell, when cast, allows you to communicate rather easily with your ancestors even if you are not at your ancestor's altar. You must come into this ritual with a specific topic or question you want to discuss.

Materials

- Earth element offerings (meat, milk, water, and wine make good offerings)
- Graveyard pine or cedar incense
- 1 Abalone shell
- 8 Blue candles
- Crystal of your choice (if you know your ancestor's birthstone, use it)
- salt

Steps

1. Creating your own invocation is the best way because you know what you are trying to accomplish and should have the specifics. Here is an example of a basic invocation just to give you an idea. Include the names of the ancestors you want to invoke.

   Ancestors living so wild and free,

Keep these gifts that come from me.
I am inviting the most special one.
To sit with me until we are done.

2. This spell works best if you're out in nature. Your backyard is okay, but the more natural and wilder the area the more the essence of your ancestor can talk to you.
3. Create a sacred circle with your 8 blue candles burning around you.
4. Surround your candles with a circle of salt.
5. Light your incense.
6. Put your offering near the candles. It is their fire that delivers the offering.
7. Sit in a comfortable position, holding your crystal, and begin your unique ancestor invocation.
8. Visualize aspects related to your ancestry and start to say the name of the ancestor you are calling for a minimum of 8 times.
9. Meditate with closed eyes and pay close attention to sounds around you. The answers come in many forms, so focus and notice any sounds or approaching animals. Or you can listen closely for the answer to come to your mind as a feeling or a decision.
10. When you feel answered, slowly open your eyes.

11. Look for responses from what you can see. You will know with your intuition what they are.
12. Close your circle and make sure to clean up afterward.
13. If the land belongs to you or the offering is biodegradable, you can leave it there. Otherwise dispose of it properly or burn it.
14. Put the crystal on your altar.
15. Continue to look for symbols and signs (feathers, dreams, rocks, unexpected phone calls) related to your ancestors throughout the day and on your way home.
16. Communication can last up to three or more days.

"I Need Closure" Spell

There really isn't a notable factor in what provides us with a feeling of closure. If it is after the loss of a loved one, we have societal bereavement displays like wearing black, funeral ceremonies, and "sitting shiva." But healing has to take place within us before we can move on and gain our peace of mind back. This spell is for closure after a loss or a breakup. It also works for any situation that has come to an end, such as a court case or graduation. It takes only around 25 minutes.

Materials
- I Bowl or cauldron of water
- Vanilla
- Rosemary
- 3 Teaspoons of Epsom salts
- Garnet or rose quartz crystal

Steps
1. In your mind's eye, visualize a doorway with a dark corridor leading away from it, while cupping the crystal in your hands.
2. Imagine the door slowly closing and speak aloud:

   This is just a passage,
   Not a place to keep.
   This is where no one goes.
   This door is now and forever closed.
   So Mote it be.

3. Stir the herbs and salt in a counterclockwise fashion into the cauldron.
4. Place your crystal in the cauldron and leave it there for 15 minutes.
5. Remove the crystal from the cauldron, take it far from your home to a crossroad, and bury

it. You can also throw the stone as far away from you as you can and you will have closure, but burying it seals the deal.

Sea Sage Cleansing

As we age, so do our homes, and over time, negative energy can build up. Consider that every argument, physical illness, bad mood, and any other negative happenings lead to the "bad juju" airing around your home and property. So, whether you have lived in your home for many years, or just moved in, it's best to stick to the old rule of "cleanliness is next to godliness." This is a tried-and-true method for keeping your surroundings happy, healthy, and negativity free!

Steps

1. Firstly, start with taking a spiritual bath or shower yourself. It is not an absolute necessity, as you have to smudge yourself anyway, but it is the best way to improve your magic.
2. Smudge yourself first. Speak aloud:

   Smoke of sage encompasses me, casting away negativity.

3. Smudge each room of the home. Repeat the chant at the back door and front door of your home with the door open while making a sweeping out motion with your hands.
4. Go back to the room where you began and start salting the home. Sea salt or regular salt works.
5. Sprinkle the salt starting with the corners and outer walls.
6. Repeat the chant in every corner and keep chanting until you salt-circle the home and finish at the back or front door.
7. Say the final chant:

So Mote it be.

Invocation of Hecate

This spell is to invoke Hecate, the ancient goddess of witchcraft, magic, necromancy, night and moon. For us, her name itself is a symbol of empowerment, mystery, and magic and causes deep rumbling within our very souls. She has a complex history, also known as the Keeper of the Keys that open the doors to our souls, and the Breaker of Chains to break whatever ties bind us. Invoking Hecate during times of struggle or stress feels uniquely supportive. This spell is to call upon

Hecate to break the chains that bind you and open the door to your soul.

Materials
- 1 Key
- 2 White candles
- Torches
- Sage
- Bay leaf
- Frankincense
- Myrrh
- Fruit
- Nuts
- Smoked fish (optional)

Steps
1. This spell is best done out in nature and on the ground, where the earth is exposed.
2. Cast a sacred circle.
3. Light two white candles on each side of your sacred circle.
4. Place your offerings next to one of the candles.
5. Next to the other candle, place the key.
6. Put the herbs over the key.

7. Pick up the key and hold it over your heart.
8. Chant while holding the key to your heart:

   I call upon you Hecate, Breaker of Chains, Keeper of Keys to bless this night with a sacred rite
   and bind your wisdom with this key, that I may wear for eternity.

9. Put the key around your neck and partake in ½ of the offering, symbolizing breaking bread with the Goddess Hecate.
10. Raise one of the candles toward the East with your left hand while waving your right hand over the earth and chant:

    most faithful Hekate, goddess of night,
    who knows my secrets and my plight
    and comes to help me with my spells
    accept my offering that from within me dwells.

11. Turn this ritual into a party or a feast. Use only natural light, play music, dance, do magic! Let your happiness shine in front of Hecate and any other gods, goddesses, or spirits who decided to attend. There is no need to close the circle because you want the spirit(s) invoked in this ritual to wander your home with their wisdom and protection.

Invocation of Nyx

As the Goddess of the night, Nyx lives in the depths of the underworld of Hades. She perfectly personifies the night, as she is a shadowy figure and has been depicted as winged, crowned, and as a charioteer. She is unique in that she can influence humans in both good ways and bad. It is said that Nyx was the only goddess feared by Zeus because she was stronger and older than him. She is honored by the crystal Moonstone and she should be called upon during a full moon. Nyx is associated with all things about the night.

Materials

- Sage
- Black salt (you can burn a stick and use the ashes to make black salt)
- White tealight candles
- 1 Purple candle
- 1 Green candle (earth)
- 1 Blue candle (water)
- 1 Yellow candle (air)
- 1 Red candle (fire)
- Myrrh incense

Steps

1. Cast your circle with candles.
2. Place the purple candle in the middle, as it represents Nyx.
3. Call the elements.
4. Light the purple candle.
5. Call out:

   Nyx of the Night, come to me!

6. When you feel her presence start to chant or sign the invocation:

   Because of you I see the night through.
   Because of you I sleep the night through.
   Because of you I cherish the night.
   Because of you I am safe and sound in the darkness.
   It is you, the Goddess of the Night,
   That has me rest easy in the darkness.
   It is you, oh Goddess of the night,
   that sees me through my darkest times.
   I thank you, oh sweet Goddess of the Night,
   for all of your blessings and your might.

7. Thank each element and close your circle.

Bonding with a Familiar

You have probably been raised to believe that most witches have black cats as pets. In reality, witches bond with a specific animal that they have a spiritual and personal connection with. Often, the familiar lives with the witch and is helpful in crafting spells and providing spiritual favors. The Native American also refers to familiars as a species of animal the practitioner has certain traits in common with. Your familiar should symbolize something inherent to you. Something you know down deep about yourself that cannot be explained but is understood by your familiar is included in this bond. For instance, rather than your pet dog sharing an inherent trait with you, maybe a wolf does. Shy people might prefer a turtle or cat, while more assertive people might better identify with bulls or oxen. People who very much enjoy nighttime activities may feel strongly connected to owls or bats. For the sake of this book, let's talk about bonding with animals that are domesticated. I wouldn't want anyone to get hurt trying to interact with wild animals, nor do I want the animal hurt or removed from its natural habitat.

Choosing your Familiar

This is a very serious matter so please take into careful consideration if you have the money, the time, and the commitment it takes to train a familiar. Having said that, it is an incredibly rewarding spiritual relationship. First off, your main obligation is to give the animal a safe and optimal quality of life, so think about practicalities. More often than not, you will be chosen by an animal familiar. Rather than going and looking for a familiar, try putting your intention out there and see who comes along.

How to Call a Familiar

1. Cast a sacred circle and light candles and incense.
2. Take your pulse to find your rhythm.
3. Beat on a drum to match the rhythm of your heart so that the familiar that may come along knows your rhythm. Do this for 5 minutes.
4. Now that the energy is raised, chant in beat with your heart:

   I call upon a beast.
   A beast calls upon me.
   We will dance together,

to the beat of our hearts.
Feather, scale, skin, or fur,
Come to me, my familiar!

5. Stop hitting the drum with the last words of the chant and imagine the animal.
6. If nothing happens, be patient. You may have a dream or a random animal may cross your path; just keep your intention open.

Once you think you have met a good option as a potential "candidate" here are some activities to deepen your relationship:

1. Try synchronizing the rhythm of your breathing by letting your animal get close enough (using common sense of course). For instance, if it is a cat, you can let the familiar sit on your chest so you can see and feel the rhythm of its breathing. Then try to match your rhythm of breathing. This is how you sync your energies and gain a better understanding of your familiar empathetically.
2. Use your crystals to soothe your familiar. It shouldn't replace regular veterinary care, but their healing energies can't hurt. It's also a great way to practice your skills.

3. If your familiar is a cat or a dog, take it on a nature walk. Make sure to use a leash, as required. It will be great for you both.
4. Use your familiar's fur or shedding in your spells. It will greatly enhance your magic because they belong to a being that you care so much for.
5. Adorn your familiar with crystals and sigils in their collar. Cast a protection spell on the collar by letting it charge in the moonlight or smudging it. Rosemary smudging is a great protective barrier with high vibrational energy.
6. Include your familiar in your sacred circle. First, try waiting for it to enter on its own or call it in. Remember, it is here for you to learn from it, not the other way around.
7. Conduct a sacred massage or use kitchen witchery on the familiar's food.
8. Once you have bonded, conduct a dedication ritual.

CHAPTER THREE:
RED MAGIC SPELLS HOODOO

Red magic is a very potent type of spell work as it involves intense emotions, passion, attention seeking, sexuality, and lust. It also works well for helping you through a bad breakup and boosting your confidence. However, remember that red is also the color of violence and rage and therefore should be practiced respectfully and carefully (Greenwood, 2014).

What is Hoodoo/Folk Magic

Folk magic includes various types of magical practices from many diverse perspectives that are connected only by the fact that they are practiced by common folk. They are not necessarily ceremonial rituals practiced by the more experienced witches. It is usually pragmatic by nature, designated to tend to the common ills of society, such as love, luck, healing, banishing, finding lost people or items, blessing the harvests, granting parenthood or fertility, and so on. Folk magic employs often simple ways that change over time. Materials used are readily available, such as twine, crystals, feathers, coins, herbs, nails, eggs, and plants.

Hoodoo is a type of black magic that started during the nineteenth century. It is a mixture of European, Native American, and African folk magic. It is commonly strongly rooted in Christian imagery. Christian Bible phrases are commonly used in magical rituals, and the Bible itself is thought of as a powerful item, capable of driving away negative forces. Hoodoo is also known as Rootwork, and despite sounding similar, it has nothing to do with Voodoo or Vodou.

American folk magic includes the Pow-Wow. Native American in origin, Pow-Wow is practiced by the people from the Pennsylvania Dutch communities. Also known as hex-work, Pow-Wow uses hex signs. These are also available to buy as trinkets, but don't have any magical power. Pow-Wow is usually practiced for protection. Often hex signs are placed on barns for protection from danger. Pow-Wow also uses Christian concepts. Mary and Jesus invocations are commonly used in incantations.

Here are the properties of red magic:

- Its Season is summer.
- It is associated with the number 1.
- Its zodiac Sign is Aries.
- Its planet is Mars.
- It is a fire element.
- Its direction is south.
- Its day is Tuesday.
- Holidays associated with it are Yule, Beltane, and the Lunar New Year.
- Its animals are the lion, tiger, wolf, and bear.
- Its crystals are all the red stones: rubies, red tourmalines, red topazes, garnets, red jaspers.
- Its magical uses include sexuality, passion, lust, all things related to blood and healing, transformation, and action, among others.

"Love Bell" Spell

A witch's bell is a force to be reckoned with! Bells are used to invoke the Elements and various deities. Spirits of evil flee from the high-pitched clear sounds bells make, especially when sounded with intent. Where you find your bell(s) is up to your intuition. You can buy a new one or look for a used one at a garage sale. It's nice to have many bells with differing tones, but for this "Love Bell" Spell, you only need one. Friday is the day of Venus, so it is the best day to cast this spell. You also want to cast this spell when there is a new moon or a full moon. This is when love spells are at their most potent.

Materials

- Witch's Bell
- 2 pink candles
- Pink rose petals
- 1 Garnet Crystal
- 1 Rose Quartz Crystal
- Palo Santo smudging bundle

Steps

1. Imagine a clear picture of who you want to cast this spell upon. Meditate on it for a while. There are many witches who have haphazardly cast love spells just to turn around and try to undo them.
2. Place your candles with the rose quartz and garnet crystals in the middle.
3. Light the candles.

4. Light your Palo Santo bundle and place it in a fireproof dish or abalone shell.
5. Pass your bell over the candle and through the smoke.
6. Ring the bell three times
7. Chant:

   Bells are ringing for Aphrodite tonight.
   Crystals of love shimmering bright.
   I cast this spell, red with fire,
   Bring the love my heart desires.
   So Mote it be/

8. Ring the bell three times each day for a week, while summoning Aphrodite and repeating the chant.
9. Carry the two crystals touching each other at all times in your pocket or pouch until your desire is met.

"Love Knot" Spell

Well, what could be a more significant symbol of love than "tying the knot"! Knots have deep significance in magic, partly due to their beautiful and simple symmetry. Very often knots are used for protection spells but in this case, you will be casting a love knot spell. The key to knot magic is using a length of 9. This can be either nine inches or nine feet. Always tie an uneven number of magical knots. If you know the person with whom you are casting the love spell, you can use their birthday. The length will be represented by the month and the number of knots will be represented by the day. If your love knot spell is for longevity of marriage, you can use the wedding anniversary with the same format.

Materials and Steps

- 3 Cords of yarn or string; you can pick your favorite romantic colors: red (passion), white (purity), and pink (love).
- Tie one knot at the end of one of the cords and imagine new love coming into your life. Chant:

    Venus, Goddess of romance and love,
    Bring me love, sent from you above.
    So Mote it be.

- Braid all three pieces of yarn together while imaging your love deepening with mutual respect.
- Tie another knot and repeat the chant.
- Continue to imagine your love in-depth; think of kissing, holding each other, happiness.

- Tie another knot and then another until you have seven knots and have chanted seven times.
- You can make this into a bracelet or carry it in your pocket but keep it on you until the spell has manifested.

Love Potion #9 Passion Tea Aphrodisiac

This love potion is an herbal aphrodisiac that will nourish, excite, elevate, and sustain your sensual or sexual desires. Herbs have magical properties for physical, mental, and spiritual wellness. The healing and wellness properties of herbs include:

- Balancing hormones.
- Strengthening reproductive organs and surrounding tissues.
- Calming stress and anxiety.
- Promoting sexual stamina and vitality.
- Providing added energy.
- Exciting olfactory senses.
- Increasing fertility for both men and women.
- Nourishing the heart and liver.
- Increasing blood flow.

Before you conjure up your spell, try a single herb for two weeks to see if you notice any connection.

Remember, each herb has its own unique magical properties.

Ingredients of Love Potion #9

- 4 Organic green tea bags or chamomile tea bags
- 3 Pinches of nutmeg
- 1 Pinch of cloves
- 1 Pinch of rosemary
- 8 Fresh rose petals
- 3 Fresh mint leaves
- 3 Cups spring water
- 3 lemon leaves or 1 tablespoon fresh squeezed lemon
- Raw honey

Steps

1. Boil the spring water
2. Make sure that you do this on a Friday and there is a new moon.
3. Combine all of the ingredients in a teapot.
4. Pour boiling water over the leaves, petals, herbs and tea bags.
5. Add honey; approximately 3 tablespoons or to personal taste.
6. Let steep for 30 minutes.
7. Add honey to sweeten and chant:

By the light of the moon I brewed this tea,
For a love spell to come over me.
Love is here to ring my bell,
With love intentions I cast this spell.
So mote it be.

8. On the next Friday, make another batch of Love Potion #9 and give a cup to the person you are interested in. Love will surely follow.

"Bathing in Sensuality" Aphrodisiac Spell

Chuparosa or hummingbird oil comes from a desert shrub with tubular yellow, orange, and red flowers. It is referred to as hummingbird oil because it attracts hummingbirds to suck on its nectar. Well, that pretty much explains why it is an aphrodisiac! You can buy it online. If you just can't get your hands on it, you can use honeysuckle, lotus, or rose oil.

Ingredients

- Chuparosa or honeysuckle oil
- Himalayan pink salt
- 4 Gems; pick your partner's birthstone or use aquamarine. Remember, clear quartz crystals can substitute for all crystals.
- Lavender flower buds

Steps

1. Make your bathing room a sacred space. Place some flowers and candles around the tub and smudge the room in all corners.
2. Set your gems up around the tub.
3. As you're filling the tub, meditate on how the water is flowing and occupying space.
4. Speak aloud your intention:

   I am in the mood for some great love making.
   I am releasing all inhibitions.

5. Slowly pour in the pink Himalayan bath salts and the essential oils.
6. Gently breathe in their aroma and notice any sensations in your body.
7. Notice the change in the water when you add the salt.
8. Take a handful of lavender buds and whisper to them your intention.
9. Scatter the flower buds into the water.
10. Slip into the bathtub or hot tub.
11. Close your eyes and take in the heightened sensations.
12. Practice creative visualization of your sexual intention.
13. Wave your hand slowly through the water and envision the cleansing of your body.

14. Cross your fingers with the fingers on your other hand and put your hands over your heart.
15. Take nine deep breaths imagining the white light entering your body with each inhale.
16. Visualize your heart spilling white light outward, creating a sphere of sensuality around you. Envision your heart radiating, shining light throughout your body and outwards, creating a sphere of love and healing around you.
17. When you feel totally ready, let the water drain.
18. STAY IN the tub until all the water has left and feel the clear and empty space.
19. Leave with your body both clean and naked.
20. Express your gratitude aloud to the elements, plant spirits, and deities.
21. Make sure to drink 8 oz of fresh spring water after the ritual.
22. Ready yourself for what comes next.

Candle Carving Ritual (Scribing)

Looking for a forever soulmate or still figuring out that you have to love yourself first, before you can love another? This powerful spell is a bit complicated even though the materials are fairly simple. Please brush up on the elements' corresponding cardinal directions in the first chapter. Scribing or carving your intention on your candle involves using sigils, names, numbers, key words, among others. Once again, this spell is all about your intuition and intention. You can use the tip of your wand, a ritual knife, or a pin. Whichever instrument you choose, smudge and charge it before scribing. The key is to carve your candle with an image of something with great meaning to you or your ritual.

Materials
- 4 Red jarred candles
- 2 White jarred candles
- Scribing tool
- Rose essential oil

Steps

1. Carve into your candle words or symbols denoting your intent.
2. Meditate on your intention while carving. Below is the Sigil for attraction, but you can use any method of carving as long as you use a sacred tool.

3. Create a sacred circle in a place safe for lighting candles. Place the four red candles, one in each cardinal point.
4. Light your north candle while invoking the earth.
5. Turning clockwise, light your east candle while invoking the air.
6. Light your south candle while invoking the fire.
7. Light your west candle while invoking the water.
8. While turning back to the north, light the first white candle just to the left of you and light the other white candle just to the right of you.
9. Speak aloud your intention each time you light a candle.
10. Put one drop of rose oil into each red candle.
11. While gazing at the flames rising up and staying steady, repeat your intention.
12. Pick up a white candle in each hand and tilt them toward each other, until they fuse into

one flame; project your intention into the flame.
13. Close your circle by blowing out the candles in the reverse order they were lit (W-S-E-N).
14. Bury both white candles in the earth in an area you visit frequently. The soil will nurture your intention, bringing it to fruition.

"Letting Go of a Lover" Spell

This spell combines healing and cleansing, since you want to heal from the letting go process, as well as becoming strong enough to move ahead. This is not a quick spell, like some in this book, as letting go of a lover is one of the most challenging situations a person can face. Give yourself time to grieve and cry over your loss, as both are healing and purifying in nature. It is all a part of the letting go process and finding your way back to peace, joy, and happiness. This spell should be cast at the start of the waning moon. It takes an entire week to manifest.

Materials

- Blade
- 1 Purple pillar candle
- 2 White pillar candles

Steps:

1. Thoroughly smudge your sacred space and for best results have your candles charged either by sunlight, moonlight, crystal, or sage.
2. At your altar, place your candles in the form of a triangle with purple at the top and the two white candles at the bottom. The purple candle symbolizes your spiritual self, and the white candles symbolize you and your lover. White represents purity and will dissipate any negative energy that was between you and your lover.
3. While picturing your best qualities in your mind, light the white candle representing you. Do the same for the other candle, except remember the best about your lover, while imagining the flame burning away the worst.
4. Light the purple candle and meditate on you and your lover at your best. This will resonate deeply within you and help you to let go when you're ready. It seems like the opposite would be true but sadness, anger, and hate weigh heavily on your spiritual and emotional vibrations. If your anger and resentments are too strong at the beginning

of the spell, smudge some more, especially around your white candles.
5. When you feel grounded and calm, snuff out your candles, starting with the purple candle, then your lover's candle and, finally, your own.
6. Repeat this for seven days, and as the candles dwindle away, so will your burden; serenity and peace will take its place.

Aphrodite Sea Charm

Known as the goddess of beauty and love in Greek mythology, Aphrodite is honored by many witches today. Venus, the goddess of love, is her equivalent in Roman mythology. This wonderful spell needs to only be cast once, and then you can use it on a daily basis. Each morning dap your neck, elbows, wrists, and your ears with this concoction.

Ingredients
- 1 Small jar
- 1 ½ Teaspoons beeswax pellets
- 2 Drops rose oil
- 2 Teaspoons vitamin E oil
- ¼ Cup almond oil
- 2 Drops vanilla oil

- 2 Drops sweet orange oil
- 2 Drops vanilla oil
- ⅛ Cup fine sea salt

Steps

1. Place 2 cups of water in your cauldron or saucepan.
2. Put the heat to medium and add the almond oil and beeswax and let them melt.
3. Take out the melted ingredients and add the vitamin E and essential oils, stirring with a sacred wooden stick or blessed popsicle stick.
4. Let the balm slightly cool but not harden.
5. Stir again and add it to your small jar and let sit until completely hardened.
6. Place your jar on your altar and light a candle.
7. Call upon the Goddess Aphrodite to favor your creation, chanting:

   Aphrodite, Goddess of beauty and love, I ask that you bless my creation , as it is crafted in your honor. So mote it be.

8. Before using, rub your hands together to warm your fingers and then apply it.

"Adoration Candle" Spell

Anointing and burning red candles will put you in touch with your carnal pleasures, as the color red is associated with passion, pleasure, and love. An adoration candle will stimulate your personal power, energy, and vitality. It is also a good spell if a woman is trying to conceive. You can unleash your pure animal magnetism by casting this powerful spell. Cast in on a Friday.

Ingredients

- 2 Red candles
- Rose oil

Steps

1. Scribe your name on one of the candles and the name of your lover on the other. If you don't yet know the name of that person, scribe "beloved" or "true love."
2. Place the candles on both sides of your altar.
3. The next day at 7:00 pm scribe a love word, such as "faithful" or "devoted" on both candles.
4. Light the candles and speak your intention. Focus on your scribed word for the day. Picture yourself in the arms of that person, loving them, feeling them, and wanting them.

5. Picture the feelings being reciprocated.
6. Snuff out the candle and chant:

   So mote it be.

7. Every evening at 7:15 pm scribe another love word into the candles and move them a bit closer to each other
8. Do this for seven days.
9. On the seventh day, the candles should be closer together. Let them burn all the way down.
10. If any wax is left, scratch it up and scatter it in a place you love, while concentrating on your spell.

Hathor's Bath Ritual

Hathor was an Egyptian goddess like no other. There were more temples built to honor Hathor (2686 BC) than even the goddess Isis! She brings protection, good health, passion, and love and is symbolized by the stars and the sky. She governs water and gives birth to the morning sun. Hathor was connected to the Nile River and all water in general. If you're looking to bring more passion into your life, this is the spell to garnish a magical connection with Hathor and perform a bathing ritual in her honor.

Ingredients

- 1 Gallon Coconut Milk
- Rose oil
- Lavender oil
- Rose petals
- 1 Red candle
- 1 Pink candle
- 1 White candle

Steps

1. Place the candles near the tub and anoint them with rose oil.
2. Fill the tub with warm water.
3. Add the coconut milk and essential oils.
4. Scatter the rose petals in the water, saying:

Hathor, who lives in Thebes, hears me! I invoke thee, to come to me so I can adore and communicate with thee. O, beautiful Goddess Hathor, I thank thee for your protection. So mote it be.

Birch Bark Love Spell

Birch Bark is known as the "White Lady of the Woods,"[1] for it is a tree of great beauty and strength. Birch bark is associated with a renewal of vows and renewal of life and love because every spring it is one of the first trees to sprout new leaves. Birch is also associated with purification, fertility, and inception. Its purification properties are due to it being a natural antiseptic. Its element is water and its crystal is the emerald. Traditionally used for Wiccan Maypoles and Beltane fires, birches are the twigs of the Witch's besom.

> ***Birch into the fire goes, in sign***
> ***of what the Lady knows.***

Steps

1. Find a birch tree you can sit against; if there are none, you can buy birch bark from several witchery shops online.
2. Get to know the beautiful birch and ask its permission to peel some bark.
3. Place the bark on your altar and center your intention while waving your hand around it and smelling its scent.
4. Carry the bark with you and show it to the person you want to attract.
5. Ask them if they enjoy the aroma.
6. If they say they do not, they are not the right person.
7. If they do enjoy the aroma, it is a great way to start a conversation.

8. Be patient, as many will love the aroma, so you'll have to use your intuition to gauge the intensity of your connection with the person and the birch.

Reverse Love Spell

This Reverse Love Spell was created to undo the effect of an original love spell. This particular spell will revert the love spell to the condition that existed before it was cast.

Steps

1. Hold a mirror facing away from you and speak aloud:

   Circle of protection,
   Realm of reflection,
   May this love begone,
   Feel the magic of this charm.
   So mote it be.

2. Smudge your entire home with white sage.
3. Scatter salt around your doors and then sweep it outside.
4. Burn a black candle at both ends while standing in front of a mirror to reverse the spell.

Attraction Poppet

An attraction spell poppet is not at all difficult to make. Follow this guide and invite a bit of romance into your life with the charming attraction spell.

Materials

- Pink fabric ⅛ of a yard
- Scrap paper
- Cotton
- Scissors
- Needle
- Pink thread
- Dried rosemary, lavender, and roses

Steps

1. Either use scrap fabric or choose a fabric based on your intuition. It is best to pick a fabric that is 100% cotton. This spell poppet employs the principles of sympathetic magic and is sometimes referred to as a "Voodoo doll," but that phrase has been given a bad rap by Western culture. For this reason we will call it a spell poppet.
2. Traditionally, a spell poppet is used to fulfill positive endeavors, and in this case, your spell poppet will attract love. Much like the

child protection poppet in the last chapter, spell poppets can also draw good luck and money.

3. On your scrap paper draw the image of your poppet. Here is an example of how basic it can be, for those of you who don't enjoy sewing:

4. Cut out your drawing and outline it on your fabric.
5. Cut the shape twice or double your fabric when you cut it.
6. Sew the poppet together leaving the bottom open for stuffing.
7. Stuff your Attraction Spell Poppet with the herbs and cotton.
8. Write your intention on a piece of nice stationary and put it into the poppet.
9. Adorn your poppet with a love sigil. You can use a red marker and make it look really nice, or you can glue crystals right on to the poppet. Get creative.
10. Charge your poppet by either sleeping with it overnight, smudging it, using a full moon, placing it in a sacred circle of crystals for

several hours, or any of the other charging methods you know or learned in this book.

CHAPTER FOUR:
SORCERY/HEX SPELLS

People often ask about sorcery or black magic. In spite of all of the debates, magic is magic and really only uses colors to create spells. Hollywood, mass media, and the gaming industry have made black magic very popular. White is portrayed as good, red is portrayed as love, green is portrayed as money, blue is portrayed as calming, and black is portrayed as evil. This color-coding can be very helpful when designing your own Book of Shadows or spell casting code.

As previously stated, it is your intention that makes the magic. Some Wiccans consider black magic as spells which try to manipulate free will and can be dangerous if they return to you by the Rule of Three. As with all magic spells, you should do your homework and take care in considering your intentions. Some consider the negativity associated with black magic has racist vibes. Many of the black magic rituals are traditionally of Hoodoo, a type of African folk magic.

Ceremonial Magic

Ceremonial magic is a branch of witchery that relies predominantly on book learning. It involves complicated, precise rituals, in complex sets of relationships. Very much grounded in Judeo-Christian religiousness up until late in the 19th century, it is not uncommon for ceremonial magicians to continue to practice within that context even today. Another word for ceremonial magic is high magic. Its purpose is meant to be spiritual in nature, rather than pragmatic. It is about gaining purification, divine knowledge, attracting appropriate influences and embracing their destiny, as well as soul improvement. Currently, there is plenty of information available publicly on the beliefs and practices of ceremonial magic or high magic. However, a review of the literature states that often there is incomplete information and that it is only through practicing and serious training that the secrets of ceremonial magic can be unlocked (Ezzy, 2006, Manning, 2014).

Left and Right Hand Magic

Briefly, left-hand magic is barred by many social conventions unless it is beneficial. Harsh warnings are issued about the consequences of any practice considered to be harmful. Satanic and Luciferian practitioners consider themselves to be on the left-hand track. A practitioner of right-hand magic lives outside of social accord and ignores taboos, sometimes feeling a heightened sense of power from breaking those conventions. Only magicians who think of themselves as right-hand practitioners generally use the terminology.

Protection Spell

Here is a powerful spell to protect you from spiritual losses, especially those shed from malevolent sources.

Materials
- Turmeric capsules
- Chalice
- Mango leaves

Steps
1. Take the turmeric orally. Turmeric creates a powerful bio magnetic field around you that

is so strong that it cannot be penetrated by evil forces.
2. Fill your chalice with water and add mango leaves. Facing the east, stare into the water for 10 minutes. Keep the chalice on your altar until evening time and then pour it out in front of your home. Do this for 21 days. This protects you from the bad eye spell.

Rune of Protection

When choosing your rune for protection let your intuition help you pick either Thurisaz or Algiz. Thurisaz symbolizes Thor's hammer of power, and it represents the conscious action of defense. It will also protect your work and bring you good luck. Upside down represents uncertainty, discouragement, and resistance. Algiz symbolizes discovery and is connected to self-protection and survival instincts. Its spiritual force creates a protective shield around you and will defend you from dangers and attacks on every level of being. You decide which one you need. It is best to use the rune at night, when it is strongest. Meditate on it just before bedtime and you will sleep better and feel safe and protected. Don't forget to use runes in their upright positions and let their energies protect you and spread their protection throughout you.

Steps

1. Wear the rune as a necklace. This way your protection will be attached to your body, especially if you have to deal with a difficult person or situation. Having it touching your skin will create a shield of protection from the evil eye and negativity.
2. Create your own sigil for either Thurisaz or Algiz and carry it with you.
3. Use it in your spell or ritual practice. Keeping your rune in your hands while creating a sacred circle, cleansing an object on your altar and chanting three times the following incredibly powerful spell:

   I call upon Thurisaz or Algiz (the one your picked),
   Be my shield of protection for all harm and danger,
   Shelter me from the storms of life.
   Keep me safe.
   So mote it be.

Pepper Pentacle

Pentacle has been symbolic of witchery for over 9,000 years. The image is associated with how we interact with the word on five levels, represented by the five points on the star. The top point is the spirit symbol, and moving clockwise, each following point is a symbol of water, fire, earth, and air. The Wiccan Pentacle is always pointed upwards, as pointing it downwards (towards Hades) would make it a satanic symbol. Many witches simply hang the pentacle on their wall as a symbol of the craft. Making it yourself is a much more power-wielding magic. Putting together sticks and branches gathered from the forest or driftwood pieces gathered from the beach will harness the elements' powers and help you along your magical journey. Black pepper is used in rituals and spells to give you protection and banish negativity and negative people from your life. If you want to rid yourself of an annoying individual, or someone has caused you harm, use black pepper, which is connected to fire. When cast with a pentacle in a spell, the black pepper packs a very powerful punch of sorcery.

Materials
- Black pepper
- Sticks

- Twine or fabric
- Pen and paper
- Black candle
- 2 Pentacles; one drawn on paper and the other made naturally.

Steps

1. Gather your sticks and twigs in a natural setting such as next to a river, in the forest, on the beach, in your neighborhood, or in the desert.
2. Pick twigs or sticks that are as straight as you can find, light in weight, and the same length. Grab some extras so you can play with how they fit best into your pentagram.
3. Create a sacred circle and lay them out on the ground, forming a five-pointed star.
4. Have the fifth point oriented in an upward direction
5. Overlap and intersect the ends, reordering the sticks until they fit the way you want them to.
6. Gather some twine, using your intuition or use material that draws you to it.
7. Wrap the twine or material where the twigs intersect until tightly bound.
8. Wrap in a clockwise direction.

9. Tie the inside intersections in the center of your star, so that wherever two sticks intersect you have twine covering them.
10. Meditate on where you want to display the star (altar, garden, or some other place that you feel is your sacred space.

Steps

This spell works with just the drawn pentacle, but for an added boost of power, constructing a pentacle from things of nature is incredibly rewarding.

1. Light your black candle.
2. Draw a large pentacle on your piece of paper.
3. Write your intention in the middle of the star.
4. Create a border around the star in black pepper.
5. Drip the black candle wax over your intention until it is covered in black wax.
6. Let the candle continue to burn for at least an hour.
7. You now have a pepper pentacle sigil.
8. Leave your sigil in a sacred place where it will not be disturbed until the spell has manifested.

"Summon a Storm" Spell

Materials

- Pentagram
- 1 Clear quartz crystal or wand
- 1 White candle and lighter

Steps

1. Place the candle in the center of your altar.
2. Place your crystal or want next to your candle.
3. Light the candle.
4. Take the lighter and start at the point of water on your pentagram. Moving in a clockwise direction, stopping at each point, speak aloud the name of each of the elements.
5. Complete the first circle and then continue until your come back to the water point:
6. Chant

   I call on the Elements of nature with all of their force:

   Water, Fire, Air, and Earth! I call upon the power of water!

7. Pick up your crystal or wand and chant:

   Clouds as black at the night,
   I call upon you to show your might,
   Come here and bring your storm.

Beneath clouds formed, more water is born.
Show your strength and your thunder.
I invoke the storm, the Earth to cover.
So mote it be.

Casting A Shadow Circle

Hold your sacred dagger (athame) in your non-dominant hand and create a circle, while imagining shadows of creatures scratching and clawing at you. Imagine the dark shadowy creatures whirling around you and starting to create pressure upon your body, as their energies compress together and become colder. Feel the pressure and icy coldness from the Abyss of whence they came circling around you, darting against your skin. As they close in against your body, all of the outside is blocked by darkness. Switch your sacred dagger to your dominant hand. This is your shadow circle. Beware of the power of the energies you have created. Speak aloud your intent. Cast your spell and then close the circle by cutting it with your dagger. Once you establish a trusting relationship with the shadows you can ask for their ultimate protection.

Summoning Succubae's Lament

The spell has to be cast on a new moon.

Materials

- New Moon
- White chalk
- 5 Black candles
- 5 Obsidian crystals
- Black Salt

Steps

1. Using white chalk, create a sacred pentagram. Nothing can cross the line once drawn.
2. Outside the line of chalk, lay black salt in a circle around the pentagram
3. Place the five black candles inside of the pentagram at equal distance from each other.
4. Outside the pentagram, lay five protective black obsidian crystals around you.
5. Meditate and imagine the pentagram separating you from everything outside the circle.
6. Light the candles.

7. Lay your body within the pentagram with your legs apart and your arms straight out and summon the succubus.
8. Imagine feeling her energy and forming a shadow you can interact with.

Invocation of Lyssa

Lyssa is known to govern anger and rage and is referred to as the Goddess of Rage. It is very important to get to know Lyssa and familiarize yourself with her energy before asking her for her help. Here are the steps for invoking Lyssa and asking her to help you in how to build your rage.

Steps
1. Using white chalk, draw three large pentagrams on the ground with one on top and two next to each other beneath it, in the shape of a triangle.
2. Stand in the center of the triangle of pentagrams.
3. Meditate on why you feel anger and when the feeling of rage comes over you, summon Lyssa, chanting:

   Oh powerful Goddess Lyssa, your mother is the Nobel Nyx,

I ask of you for guidance and help as I am a child of the darkness, like you.

Rage has been gathered within my heart and I ask your help in releasing it upon those who wish to harm me. I ask of you to teach me your artistic manifestations of rage and guide me in my magic endeavors. If I am linked to you, I can accomplish anything!

4. You will know you have connected with Lyssa if you feel her presence and energy. If you don't, meditate more on your rage and try again.
5. Once you have established a relationship with Lyssa, nourish it with offerings and conversation regularly to keep her favor.

Liar's Lamentation Spell

Materials

- 4 Quarters
- 1 Onion
- 1 Cup of wine

Steps

1. Carve the liar's name on the onion.
2. Speak aloud your intention and ask the earth for help.

3. Start ripping the onion layer by layer. By doing so, you are symbolically tearing away the phony fronts of the liar that they use for deception.
4. Keep tearing until you have exposed the core of the onion, which is also the core of the liar.
5. Throw the onion outside where it can rot away. The liar's deception will rot with it.
6. Leave the 4 nickels on the ground as an offering to the earth.

A Seduction Spell

This is a very strong seduction spell that will have the person you cast it upon unable to sleep without thinking of you. It will consume them until you are together. It can also bring back a lost love you desire.

Materials
- 13 Black candles (small)
- 1 Chicken heart
- Photo or item belonging to the person with whom you are casting the spell
- Parchment paper and pencil
- Twine

Steps

1. Lay the parchment paper down flat in front of you.
2. In pencil write the following:

   Great Gods of the rushing rivers
   Rein your power down on (the person's name).
   Break them until they fall so deeply for me and if I choose so, for an eternity.
   So mote it be.

3. Create a sacred circle around the paper with the black candles.
4. Standing over and looking down on your written passage, place the item belonging to that person in the center.
5. Light one candle at a time and place of drop of each one's wax on the item, focusing intensely on your intention.
6. Place the chicken heart on top of the wax drippings.
7. Blow out each candle chanting:

   As it should be, as it is.

8. Bury the package by a tree.
9. On the next full moon, return to the tree with the 13 candles.

10. Make a circle with the candles over the burial site.
11. Light them and let them burn all the way down while you meditate on the spell.
12. Close the circle and clean up the area.

"Tattered Hearts" Spell Part I

This spell is cast to end a relationship, but Tattered Hearts Part II Spell is cast to mend one of the hearts from the ended relationship as a result of Part I.

Materials

- 2 Pieces of Heart Shaped Material. You can draw a heart on some spare fabric and cut it out.
- Needle and thread
- Sharpie
- 2 Candles, 1 black, 1 red.

Steps

1. With your sharpie, write the name of the couple, one on each heart.
2. Sew the hearts, with just a few stitches, together.
3. Light the candles and chant:

   What together is now,

Is soon torn apart.
Stars fade with time.
The couple departs.
So mote it be.

4. Rip the hearts apart.
5. Blow out the candle to finish this spell.

"Tattered Hearts" Spell Part II

This is the second part of the spell. It will bring you the person to whom you are attracted. Hopefully, you were positive about your feelings before you cast Part I.

Steps

1. Prepare a bowl of water from the sea.
2. Cast a sacred circle.
3. Take the heart of the person you want to be with from the two hearts in Part I and place it in the bowl.
4. Chant:

   I know your heart is broken;
   I am here to ease your pain.
   With darkness gone, then I come along,
   The end was not in vain.
   So mote it be.

5. Take the heart out of the sea water and put it somewhere to air dry.
6. The spell will be in effect unless you decide to break the spell by destroying the heart.
7. If that happens, burn the heart in your cauldron with the flame of a white candle.

Carman's Hex

This hex came from an old woman from Ireland. She said it is a simple hex that can be used in any spell or ritual. It sounds like a nursery rhyme, with a hex at the end.

> *"Tables, knives, chairs, forks*
> *Cups, bottles, tankards, and corks,*
> *Beds, bottles, dishes, and keg,*
> *Pudding, milk, bacon, and eggs*
> *All of the sheets on the bed*
> *The spices in cupboards and the baked bread*
> *Every provision on the shelf,*
> *All you'll have left is the house itself!"*

Binding by Fear

Materials

- Black Candle
- Lighter

- Black thread
- Photo of target or write their full name on a piece of paper
- Jar

Steps

1. Prepare your altar.
2. Light the black candle.
3. Tightly tie up the picture with the black thread, so you cannot see any of the face.
4. Chant:

   Whether far or near,
   You will feel the fear,
   You caused it you know,
   Deservedly so.
   I have the key.
   So mote it be.

5. Drip the black wax over the tied-up bundle until it touches on all sides.
6. Put the wax covered bundle in the jar.
7. Hide the jar at nighttime.

Spell to Bind a Bully

Before we even start discussing this spell, you must make sure you are binding a bully! The whole reason for casting a binding spell is to "bind someone's powers to prevent them from doing harm." The key point here is that if you use a binding spell only for protection and justice, you are safe from any negative karmic backlash. The best time to cast this spell is during a waning moon.

Materials

- Piece of paper and pen
- Black sea salt (you can use white sea salt too)
- Black thread
- Black candle

Steps

1. On a piece of paper, write the name of the bully and put it in the center of your altar.
2. Light your black candle.
3. Take your sea salt and make a circle around the bully's name moving in a clockwise direction.
4. Take your black thread and tie it around the paper, crumpling it.
5. Chant:

    (Name of the bully), I bind you.
    You are harmless to all other people and to the planet.
    Your hostility and insults are powerless.
    You can cause no harm from this day on.

So mote it be.

6. Repeat the chant six times.
7. Snuff out the candle.
8. Leave the knotted spell in the salt until morning.
9. Brush the salt onto another piece of paper and flush it down the toilet.
10. Throw the knotted paper and the bully's name into the flame.

Spell for Stopping Harassment

Materials

- Blade or athame
- Brown candle
- Honey
- Piece of parchment paper
- Pen

Steps

1. Scribe the person's name on the back and front of the brown candle.
2. In the center of the candle use your athame to dig out a pocket of wax.
3. On a small parchment paper write:

> *From this day on, (target's name)*
> *speaks only nice words about me.*
> *This spell is cast. So mote it be.*

4. Place one drop of honey in the middle of the parchment paper and ball it up.
5. Stick the balled-up paper in the dug-out pocket in the candle (imagine sticking it in the person's mouth).
6. Let the candle burn for 15 minutes every other night for nine nights.
7. Save some of the wax drippings.
8. Throw the candle into running water away from your home or hold it under running water for a few minutes and then throw it away in the outside garbage.
9. Scatter the wax drippings in the path of the person harassing you. If you don't have any wax drippings, use ash or black salt.

Sour Jar

Sour jars do exactly as their name suggests. They sour a person's life or they can be used to sour a relationship that you want to break up. All you need is a jar half-filled with vinegar and ⅛ cup of mustard seeds.

Steps

1. Take a paper with your intention written on it using the person's or people's name(s).
2. Put it in the jar.
3. Add a bunch of "yucky" stuff like rusty nails, pet shedding, broken glass, a rotten egg, etc.
4. Keep the jar for one month and then bury it outside.

Discord and Darkness Spell

This spell becomes manifested by focusing your mind on projecting chaos, so make sure you are good and angry before starting.

Materials

- Piece of black yarn
- Salt

Steps

1. Make three knots in your black yarn, place it on your altar.
2. Circle the yarn with salt.
3. Chant:

   Three knots to seal this hex,
   No sleep for you, nor any rest.
   Discord shows you to your fate.

*Knots of rage are not too late.
I tied another knot, now two,
To send the darkness over you.
A third knot, now I bind,
Spreading discord through your mind.
As it is and should be.
So mote it be.*

4. Hide the yarn where it cannot be disturbed, until you are ready to untie the knots and undo the spell.

Bad Luck Potion

Drink a cup of this potion in combination with the previous Discord and Darkness Spell to eliminate the person that is troubling your life.

Ingredients

- Smoky quartz crystal
- Dark colored glass potion bottle or jar (or you can tape black paper around the bottle when finished and use a gold ink pen to mark a sigil on the label.
- Bay leaf
- ⅛ teaspoon cayenne pepper
- Distilled water
- Black licorice extract

Steps

1. Place the smoky quartz crystal in the distilled water and leave under moonlight overnight to charge.
2. Add the rest of the ingredients.
3. Remove the crystal and bury it in black soil.
4. Store your potion in a cool dry place or in the refrigerator.

"Ring of Power" Enchantment

Materials

- Rock salt
- Black obsidian crystal ring
- Goblet with blessed water

Steps

1. Sprinkle rock salt into the goblet of blessed water.
2. Place your goblet in the center of your altar.
3. Put the ring into the goblet.
4. Chant:

   I am granted the power in my hands
   From Sea, Air, Fire, and Land.
   The Goddess and Elements give power to me,
   With this spell, the more powerful I'll be.

So mote it be.

5. After three hours, remove the ring and put it on a finger of your dominant hand.
6. Wear the ring for nine days without letting anyone touch it.
7. Repeat the spell every day for nine days while rubbing the crystal.
8. Feel and acknowledge the powerful feelings entering your body.
9. Give thanks to the elements and goddess with an offering on your altar.

Effigy Poppet Curse

Materials

- Black fabric
- Paper and pen
- Black thread and needle
- Black candle
- Graveyard dirt
- Tobacco
- Cayenne Pepper
- Black Salt
- Black obsidian crystal

Steps

1. Do this by the light of a black candle.

2. Write your target's name on a piece of paper.
3. Cut your poppet out of the fabric; cut two matching pieces.
4. Sew it together leaving the top open for stuffing.
5. Place all of your ingredients into the poppet and sew closed.
6. Carry your poppet and black candle to your altar and whisper your hex in its ear:

Whatever happens to this poppet, you will feel too.
"Person's name" is this poppet, this poppet is you.
My whisper to this poppet, you will know it's true.
As you are this poppet and this poppet is you.
So mote it be.

"Nightmare Jar" Spell

Materials

- 1 small jar with top
- Black sharpie
- Black candle
- Black salt
- Black yarn (8 inches)

- Lock of hair from the target you want to protect or your own
- 10 Rusty nails
- 10 Pieces of broken glass
- Mint leaves
- Bay leaves

Steps

1. Light your candle.
2. Place the lock of hair into the jar.
3. Place nails and broken glass in the jar.
4. Add the herbs.
5. Add ½ of your black salt imagining it sucking the negative energy from your target into the darkness to remain forever. Picture a black hole with the nightmares speeding into it.
6. Pour in the rest of your salt.
7. Put 20 drops of candle wax in the jar.
8. Write the name of the target on a piece of white paper with the sharpie.
9. Put it into the jar.
10. Add 10 drops of candle wax on top of the name of the person.
11. Seal the jar.
12. Place the jar under the moonlight for charging.
13. Keep the jar in a window for continuous charging to banish the nightmares.

"Banishing Your Ex" Hex

Sometimes exes just won't go away and will continue to make our lives miserable. If you have tried everything known to mankind to get rid of your ex, this is your next step. Make sure you want to be rid of this person for good and that you are not just temporarily angry.

Materials

- Picture of your ex
- Pen
- Paper
- Black candle
- White candle
- Sage
- Abalone shell

Steps

1. Open all of the windows and turn on any fans in the house.
2. Light the white candle.
3. Start burning your sage and chanting while walking around and cleansing your entire house, waving in a clockwise direction. Cover every corner, every window, and every door, repeating the chant:

> *I purge myself of (ex's name) and all of their negativity.*
> *So mote it be.*

4. As you watch the smoke fly out of the windows, imagine the smoke taking your ex with it.
5. Write your ex's name on the piece of paper.
6. Imagine your life with your ex no longer in it.
7. Burn the paper.
8. As quickly as it burns, take the ashes outside and toss them to the wind.

"You're so Vain and Insane" Hex

This spell is for a person who is so vain they don't even think about anyone else. Once cast, they will lose their vanity when they look in the mirror.

Materials

- Item belonging to target
- Black marker
- Black candle
- Flammable poppet
- Fireproof bowl or cauldron

Steps

1. Go outdoors.
2. Take the item belonging to your target.
3. Write the target's name on the poppet with the black marker.
4. Put the poppet in the cauldron and ignite it and chant:

(Target's name), for all to see,
Begone your feelings of vanity.
You will see yourself like others do.
Begone all vanity now from you.
So mote it be.

Business Butcher Curse

1. Relax and take some time to meditate on the nasty workings of the business you are going to curse.
2. Draw a red circle on a piece of paper.
3. Focus on a specific issue that draws you in and ask yourself "who or what is the cause for this situation?"
4. You will most likely come to a conclusion about which entity or entities are causing you or yours harm or distress.
5. Write the name of the business in the middle of the red circle.
6. Focus your intention on how much better things will be without the organization.

7. Either use tape or a glue stick and stick it somewhere on the building of the business where it cannot be seen.
8. Feel good that you have now conducted your first tactical magic spell!

Poppet Curse of Slight Pain

This spell is for that person you wish you could just slap or punch because of all the pain they've caused you. Fortunately, with this spell, you can do just that.

Materials

- Poppet (use the method from the earlier poppet spell or carve a person's name in a bar of soap)

Steps

1. Hold your poppet in your dominant hand and slowly grip it tighter. After focusing on your rage toward the target, drop it on the floor.
2. Your poppet is now charged and ready to do magic
3. You can now punch it or thump it on the arm.

4. The stronger your intention, the more harm that can be inflicted.

"Agony of Acne" Curse

Materials

- A small item with your target's DNA on it
- Grime and dirt
- 1 small vile
- 1 Black Candle
- 1 Red Candle

Steps

1. Put the DNA in the vile.
2. Put the grime and dirt in the vile.
3. Drip wax from both candles in the vile.
4. Bury the vile in your target's yard.

"Evil Eye" Enchantment

The belief in the evil eye curse goes back to cave drawings from over 10,000 years ago that were discovered in Spain. It is believed that a person will cast an evil eye with a certain glare in their eyes to someone who is vain, bragging about their wealth, showing no respect for others, or gossiping. Wearing a glass evil eye symbol will reflect back any malicious intent onto the caster. The curse can cause a number of ailments that can range from small annoyances to major catastrophes. The ritual to cast off or remove the curse of the evil eye is through releasing the negative vibrations instilled in the curse. The evil eye is composed of black energy that affects a person's mental, emotional, and spiritual realms.

Steps to Ward Off the Evil Eye

1. Wearing jewelry depicting the evil eye will protect you from the curse and reflect it back on the person who cast it.
2. Write down on a piece of paper "buri nazar wale tera muh kala" ("O evil-eyed one, may your face turn black") and carry it in your wallet.
3. Using wall hangings of the evil eye will protect you and your home.
4. Sweep a raw egg over your body or the body of the person cursed. Break the egg into a glass of blessed water and put it under the head of the bed of the cursed person.

5. Phallic charms to ward off evil have been practiced for centuries.

CHAPTER FIVE:
RUNE CASTING & DIVINATION

Some of the Wiccan practitioners' divination is achieved by casting runes. Similar to Tarot card readings, casting runes is not about predicting the future or fortune-telling, so to speak. Rather, it is an enlightenment tool that works in conjunction with your subconscious to help with problem-solving and possible outcomes. While sometimes you may come across obscure meanings, most people have learned to be specific with their questions and base them on their current circumstances. Rune casting has been around since ancient Roman times and appears again in the Norse Sagas and Eddas. While you can buy runes that are pre-made, creating your own puts more of your own energy into them.

The term for making your own runes is "risting." Historically, runes were made from nut-bearing trees or pine, hazel, oak, or cedar. You can burn, carve, or paint the symbols on your runes. Some people paint stones and top them with acrylic to keep the symbols from rubbing off with use. Risting runes is part of their magical properties and should only be done when you achieve enough knowledge and proper preparation. Furthermore, using a white colored cloth to cast your runes upon makes it easier for you to cast them. However, some people prefer to cast runes on the ground. Keep runes stored in a sacred pouch or box when you are not using them.

TIWAZ (Tyr)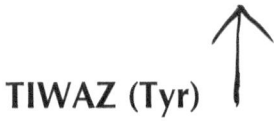

TIWAX is the rune of justice and balance. It is ruled by higher rationality and is the rune of self-sacrifice to the best interest of others and society as a whole. It is associated with fairness, keeping the peace, and the rule of law.

Letter in the alphabet: 23

Color: Bright red

Element: Air

Tree: Oak

Herb: Sage

Crystals: Garnet, jasper, topaz, citrine, ruby, and bloodstone

Animals: Hawk, owl, bear, falcon, and hound

Energy: Sacrifice, appropriate decision making, supreme order, honor, warrior, and righteousness.

Magical Use: Loyalty, analysis, honesty, rationality, faith, victory, self-sacrifice and over-sacrifice.

Divinations: honesty, faith, loyalty, justice, rationality, self-sacrifice, analysis, victory OR defeat, injustice, overly sacrificing and tyranny.

BERKANO (Birch Goddess)

The Birch Goddess or BERKANO rune is all about renewal and rebirth. It governs gardening and is known as the Earth Mother and the rune of becoming. Its energy is associated with plant life, trees, and female fertility. The Birch Goddess is healing and connected to the womb and raising children.

Letter in the alphabet: 18

Color: Dark green

Element: Earth

Tree: Birch

Herb: Lady's mantle

Crystals: All

Animals: All

Energy: Wisdom, silence, dependence, and safety

Magical Uses: Metabolism and excretion, harmony, strengthens powers of secrecy, openness, creativity, and dance.

Divinations: Sanctuary, changes in life, becoming, confidence, shelter, secrets, birth OR sterility, insecurity, and deceit.

EHWAZ (Horse) M

EHWAZ or Horse is the rune of trust and teamwork, which refers to two entities together working toward the same goal. It is also the rune of sexuality.

Letter in the alphabet: 19

Color: Red

Element: Earth

Tree: Yew

Crystal: Topaz

Herb: Ragwort

Animal: Horse

Energy: Cooperation and trust, friendship, and animals.

Magical uses: An entity who is within you and with you in all of your incarnations is known as The Fetch. EHWAS activates your Fetch. Also known as the horse, this rune helps you bond with all animals (horse whisperer), allowing you to uncover deceit quickly.

Divinations: Marriage and teamwork, a friend, loyalty, harmony, trust OR disharmony, mistrust, nightmares, an enemy, indecision, and betrayal.

MANNAZ (Mankind)

MANNAZ is the rune of mind, learning, and memory. It is the humanitarian rune. Invoking MANNAZ provides you with entry into humanity and Earth's collective unconscious.

Letter of the alphabet: 20

Color: Red

Element: Air

Tree: Holly

Crystal: Garnet

Herb: Madder

Animal: Man

Energy: Transformation from past lives, dreams, and the unconscious

Magical Uses: Self-actualization, raises intelligence, higher self-awareness, mental powers and memory (perfect if you need to pass a test), unlocks the mind's eye (the third eye), acknowledgment of the divine structure in all beings, spiritual and mental potential.

Divinations: Intelligence, social order, sustainability, awareness, driving influence, OR bigotry, elitism, blindness, depression, arrogance, and mortality.

LAGUZ (Water)

The LAGUZ rune is associated with hidden powers, change, and the sea. This rune refers to your intuition powers, and the listening skills necessary to live a life of complete freedom.

Letter of the alphabet: 21

Colors: Orange, Blue, Dark green

Element: Water

Tree: Willow

Crystal: Pearl

Herb: Amaranth

Animal: Otter and seal

Energy: The spirit of the sea, the astral plane, unity in love, life energy, evolution, and the origin of life

Magical uses: Change, empathy, increased energy, dreams, mystery, collective unconscious, and the ability to adapt. Primal fears and insecurities.

Divinations: Memory, dreams, vitality of the sea, fantasy, growth, circular motion, OR depression, emotional blackmail, withering, avoidance, lack of morality, poison, manipulation, and toxicity.

INGWAZ or INGUZ (Seed)

The INGWAZ OR INGUZ has great power and symbolizes a new path in your life, or a new life. It will shed enough strength to reach a resolution, which results in a fresh start. INGUZ governs transformational power in ritual use and how to center your thoughts and energy through passive meditation .

Letter of the alphabet: 22

Colors: Gold, orange, yellow, green

Elements: Water and earth

Tree: Willow

Crystal: Amber

Herb: Self-heal

Animal: Boar

Energy: Mysteries of the male, earth-god, process of gestation, energy storage

Magical uses: Inner-child, personal growth, wholeness, powers of suggestion.

Divinations: Personal growth or immaturity, self-care OR frivolity, gestation or impotence, expectation or inability to change.

DAGAZ (Dawn) ᛞ

The DAGAZ rune, meaning Dawn, governs the ability to become invisible and receive the gift of mystical inspiration. It has the ability to transform things into their opposite state as it integrates the male and female into one being who feels complete.

Letter of the Alphabet: 14

Colors: Blue, light blue, yellow, orange, and red

Element: Fire

Tree: Spruce

Crystal: Peridot and diamond

Herb: Mullein

Animal: Raven, wolf, eagle, and bear

Energy: Represents the light at dawn and at dusk, synthesis, unity, transmutation, and non-dual reality

Magical uses: Self-esteem, truth, perseverance, hospitality, loyalty, honor, industriousness, courage, truth, and honor.

Divinations: Hope and happiness, awareness, paradigm shift, the ideal, and awakening OR insomnia, hopelessness, catastrophic change.

RAIDHO (Riding)

RAIDHO symbolizes life's journey and is connected to the inner-self and the daylight. It will take you down the right path with nobility and merit.

Letter of the Alphabet: 5

Colors: Bright red, blue, and dusty brown

Element: Air

Tree: Oak

Crystal: Chrysoprase

Herb: Mugwort

Animal: Pack animals and horse

Energy: Rhythm active presence, and cosmic cyclical law

Magical Uses: Transportation, adventure, counsel, moral compass, integrity, rituals, initiative, nobility, control of oneself, celestial procession, and the right action.

Divinations: Justice, journey, action, sound advice, ordered growth, OR stasis, irrationality, restlessness, crisis, rigidity, wrongful imprisonment, hypocrisy, and control freak.

KENAZ (Torch)

KENAZ symbolizes intellect, knowledge, mastery of fire, creation, and cremation. It governs ability, magic, and art.

Letter of the Alphabet: 6

Colors: Red, white, pink, blue, grey, red-golds, brown, and yellow.

Element: Fire

Tree: Pine

Crystal: Bloodstone

Herb: Cowslip

Animal: Dragon

Energy: Learning-teaching dynamic, transformation, and illumination

Magical Uses: Skills, creativity, craftsmanship, intuition, quest for truth, intellect and knowledge, playfulness, study, opportunity, occult female secrecy, cunning.

Divinations: Craft, offspring, ability, transformation, OR decay, ignorance, elitism, breakup, disease, lacking creativity, and inability.

GEBO (Gift) X

Each decision made in life requires an acceptance with a simultaneous release or sacrifice. It tells you that something good is coming your way that might be money or it might be love.

Letter of the Alphabet: 7

Colors: Rose and deep blue

Element: Air

Tree: Elm and ash

Crystal: Opal

Herb: Eucalyptus

Animal: Owl

Energy: Sacrifice, resolving barriers by the act of gift giving, and exchanged powers.

Magical Uses: Generosity, hospitality, obligations, contracts, dept, favors, and taking an oath.

Divinations: Gifting, sacrifice, generosity, honor, divine vision OR greed, dependence, dishonesty, moodiness, and loneliness.

WUNJO (Joy)

WUNJO surrounds the principles of ecstasy and joy, as well as inner harmony. It is about family, bonding, shared identity, and cooperation. It symbolizes our inner-child and makes for a happy couple.

Letter of the Alphabet: 8

Colors: Indigo, blue, yellow, light blue, light green

Element: Earth

Tree: Ash

Crystal: Diamond

Herb: Flax

Animal: Wolf

Energy: Fellowship, friendship, harmony, effortlessness, wishing, and harmony of like forces

Magical Uses: Shared identity, optimism, contentment, family, parties, friendship, goal achievement, enlightenment, and hope.

Divinations: Accomplishment, harmony, prosperity, fellowship OR strife, betrayal, stupidity, alienation, and deception.

HAGALAZ (Hail)

HAGALAZ or Hail is a powerful rune, symbolizing spiritual fulfillment and protection. It is associated with your dreams and emotions as a cleansing agent. HAGALAZ governs regression, acceptance, and psychoanalysis.

Letter of the Alphabet: 9

Colors: Indigo, dark brownish green, grey, black and bright green.

Elements: Earth and water

Tree: Ash

Crystal: Onyx

Herb: Lily-of-the-Valley

Animal: Falcon, owl, whale, wolf, eagle, hawk, vulture, and dolphin

Energy: Superhuman powers, violent natural forces, seed forming, chaos, and the ability to confront someone objectively

Magical Uses: Transformation, confrontation, banishing spells for protection, awakening the subconscious of others through brutal honesty.

Divinations: Changes for the long run goals, crisis management, inner harmony, completion, and corrections; OR crisis, stagnation, property loss, blame, stuck in the past, victimization, catastrophe, disappointment, obsessing about the past.

NAUTHIZ (Necessity)

NAUTHIZ is the rune of fate, constriction, relief and vital fire. It governs acceptance, magical ability development, and overcoming distress. This rune is great energy for generating problem-solving abilities and for protecting your own needs. This is the rune for love spells.

Letter of the Alphabet: 10

Colors: Dark Red and black

Element: Fire

Tree: Beech

Crystal: Lapis lazuli

Herb: Bistort

Animal: Cow

Energy: Urgency, coming forth, and necessity.

Magical Uses: Stress management, protection, hard work, chores, summoning the Sun's power, and cleansing.

Divinations: Recognition of primal truth, innovation, strength in resistance, personal growth, self-reliance, and life lessons; OR distress, worry, cowardice, guilt, drudgery, toil, warnings and unfulfilled needs.

ISA (Ice)

ISA is the rune of being in a frozen or static state and of concentration. It governs the ego and a state of stillness. It is associated with self-mastery. From ISA we learn that death is part of life.

Letter of the Alphabet: 10

Colors: Black, white, pale and bright blue

Element: Water

Tree: Alder

Crystal: Cat's eye

Herb: Henbane

Animal: Polar bear

Energy: Frozen, stillness, stasis, and contraction

Magical Uses: Protection, freezes negative forces from entering your space, power over unwanted outbursts, defense and destruction.

Divinations: Self-control, unity, self-care OR dullness, psychopathy, egomania, immobility, and blindness.

ANSUZ (Speech)

ANSUZ or the speech rune governs the cognitive senses and speech. It will mentally inspire you. ANSUZ is associated with a baby's first breath and the last breath before death. ANSUZ transmits magical powers from generation to generation, giving way to the truth that there is no divide between us and the universe.

Letter of the Alphabet: 4

Colors: Sky blue, grey, and dark blue.

Element: Air

Tree: Ash

Crystal: Emerald

Herb: Fly Agaric

Animal: Raven and wolf

Energy: Communication, answers, sovereign ancestral god, spirit, and exploration

Magical Uses: Communion, listening, inspiration, and stability.

Divinations: Intellect, open communication, power in words, transformation, OR bad advice, misunderstanddings, delusions, and being easily manipulated.

THURISAZ (Thorn)

THURISAZ is symbolic of Thor's hammer. It is associated with the consciousness of the Warrior and matters requiring wisdom with force. It is about being the ultimate force in fighting for freedom for all human beings. If you want to combat blockages in your spirit, mind and body, THURISAZ is the rune to cast.

Letter of the Alphabet: 3

Colors: Dark and bright red, white, grey, and purple

Elements: Fire and water

Tree: Thorn and oak

Crystal: Sapphire

Herb: House Leek

Animal: Raven, crow, and wolf

Energy: Chaos, empowerment, resistance breaker, violent storms, forces of defense, and enthusiasm

Magical Uses: Struggles with your unconsciousness, enthusiasm, sexual prowess, masculinity, and creating boundaries.

Divinations: Direct force, conflict resolution, reactive force, regeneration, OR betrayal, disease, combative violence, annoyance, dullness, and defenselessness.

OTHALA (Homeland)

OTHALA (ODAL), or the rune of the homeland, governs over fences. It governs over ancestral spiritual powers, property, and divine inheritance. It helps us figure out our societal role. If you're looking for some wise advice, OTHALA is the place to ask for it.

Letter of the Alphabet: 23

Colors: Red, brown, dark yellow,

Elements: Earth

Tree: Hawthorn

Crystal: Ruby

Herb: Clover

Animal: Beaver

Energy: Paradise, inheritance, ancestral spiritual powers, utopia, and heaven on earth

Magical Uses: Collects knowledge and powers from generations past, wealth of property, deserved inheritance from ancestors, comprehension of global unity, safety, security, royalty, and protection.

Divinations: Freedom, prosperity, estate or home, group order, productive interactions OR homelessness, slavery, xenophobia, totalitarianism, lack of order, genocide, and poverty.

JERA (Year)

JERA or the Year rune represents the union between heaven and earth, the life cycle, the sun's cycle, and the eternal return. It governs peace in the heart and on land, naturally ordered actions, and harvest. It is associated with planning for the future. Like the sleep cycle, dawn to dusk, JERA signifies the heartbeat and the breath.

Letter of the Alphabet: 12

Colors: Red gold, black, brown, green, and light blue

Elements: Earth

Tree: Oak

Crystal: Cornelian

Herb: Rosemary

Animal: Firefly

Energy: Orbits, biorhythms, good harvest, good effort, and progress

Magical Uses: Creativity, prosperity, peace, fertility, harmony, and plenty. Invoking the power of the cycles and times, brings to you the acknowledgement of the universe's cyclic nature. Brings intention into manifestations and initiates a lasting but gradual change in the flow of life.

Divinations: Plenty, good timing, being rewarded from positive action, peace OR conflict, bad timing, repetition, poverty, and regression.

EIHWAZ or IHWAZ (Yew Tree)

EIHWAZ or IHWAZ, the rune of the Yew Tree and of the secrets of life and death. This rune suggests the opportunities that come when you risk a different path. It is usually a sign of waiting and tells you to keep looking towards the future.

Letter of the Alphabet: 13

Colors: Red gold, black, brown, green, and light blue

Elements: Earth

Tree: Yew

Crystal: Topaz

Herb: Mandrake

Animal: Eagle, spider, eel, lizard, hound, horse, wolf, raven, serpent, dragon, jaguar, dolphin, salmon, butterfly, dragonfly, kingfish, and moth

Energy: Encoding, balancing the chakra system, and secrecy

Magical Uses: Allows you the wisdom of the chakras, and World Tree (Yggdrasil), will help you to develop your spiritual endurance, communication between different realities, and your ability to gain the initiative for any endeavor.

Divinations: In the direction of Enlightenment, initiation, protection, endurance OR weakness, destruction, confusion, dissatisfaction, and death.

PERTHRO (Unknown)

PERTHRO's true meaning is unknown, but is thought to be a rune of favorable circumstances. It is associated with the Great Goddess and therefore reflects timelessness, magical transformation, and spiritual regeneration. This rune provides you with a direction, but gives you the free will to make the right choice. It symbolizes actions and reactions and the fundamental mysteries of the universe.

Letter of the Alphabet: 14

Colors: Black, green and silver

Elements: Water

Tree: Beech

Crystal: Aquamarine

Herb: Aconite

Animal: Water moccasin, hound, falcon, hawk, and wolf

Energy: Nothingness, the unmanifested, luck and evolutionary forces

Magical Uses: Manipulate cause and effect, higher probability of luck, creates favorable circumstances, gambling, guessing, chance, and divination.

Divinations: Good luck, joy, fellowship, evolution, knowledge, OR addictions, delusions, unknowability, stagnation, and loneliness.

ALGIZ (Life)

ALGIZ is the rune of life, independence, faith, and autonomy. It will provide you with courage when facing fear. However, it does not banish fear, in case fear is spawned as a warning. It gives you the insight you need to make good judgements.

Letter of the Alphabet: 15

Colors: Black, silver, and green

Elements: Air

Tree: Yew

Crystal: Amethyst

Herb: Angelica

Animal: Deer and elk

Energy: The divine plane, teaching and protection, Valkyries from the battlefield to Valhalla

Magical Uses: Strengthens your life force through courageous acts and allows you to understand things which are not human. Religious and mystical communications with other universes, defense and protection. Banishes the fear of death. Spirituality and safety.

Divinations: Awakening higher awareness, connection with the Goddesses, higher life, protection, OR loss of the link to the divine, fear, hidden danger, and dissipation by divine powers.

SOWILO (Sun)

SOWILO or the sun rune is the force that runs counter to the rune ISA. It governs the force of fire in the mental and physical world and promotes optimism, persistence, dedication, and invigoration in all endeavors. It will guard you against the hurtful opinions of others so your heart will stay focused on your intentions.

Letter of the Alphabet: 16

Colors: Gold, blue, silver, white, yellow, and green

Elements: Fire

Tree: Juniper

Crystal: Ruby

Herb: Hedge wolf

Animal: Rooster

Energy: Strengthens chakras, life-giving force, motivation, sun-wheel, and action

Magical Uses: Transformation of thoughts into action, activates your highest value system, wellness, will guide your way to enlightenment, increase your psychic abilities, success driven by self.

Divinations: Hope, faith, purpose in life, honor, success, and goals, OR gullibility, no goals, poor advice, and false success.

FEHU (Cattle)

The Fehu or cattle rune symbolizes two cow's horns or two branches of a tree. Historically, families with many cattle were considered wealthy. Cattle was used in the past in the same fashion as money is used today. If you cast the FEHU rune, success and wealth will be arriving soon. The Fehu rune carries with it a cautionary warning. That is to use these earnings on something permanent or solid once they come. It will remind you how fast money can slip through your fingers, if you don't spend it carefully. It is associated with your goals and dreams. It may be indicating that you have debts piling up and you should be on the road to satisfying them immediately.

When inverted, Fehu references a dark side of wealth. It can symbolize corruption and can also be reminding you to be careful with your money and properties, rather than letting them control you. Money, like all things, can be used for both good and evil. It carries with it both negativity and positivity. As such, Fehu inverted references to the dark side of money.

Letter of the alphabet: 2

Color: Red

Elements: Fire and earth

Tree: Elder

Crystal: Moss Agate

Herb: Nettle

Animal: Cow

Energy: Sustainability, circulation, expansive energy

Magical Uses: Social success, travel, wealthy, fresh beginnings, generosity, foresight, power, reputation, sexual energy, fertile harvest, crisis management, luck, control, increased psychic strength, and breaking the spirit of an adversary.

Divinations: Money, foresight, fresh beginnings, travel, social success; OR failure, poverty, greed, endings, and atrophy.

URUZ (AUROCHS)

URUZ or Aurochs is a powerful rune of the unconscious, which is shaping your energies that need guided wisdom as they manifest. It is a cautionary rune, reminding you that untamed creative powers can be dangerous. This is a reality evident in our civilization's use of modern technology. It is the practitioner practiced methods and skill level that will control the energy untethered from this rune. URUZ is associated with assertiveness, independence, and one's own territory.

Letter of the alphabet: 2

Color: Dark Green

Tree: Birch

Crystal: Carbuncle

Herb: Sphagnum Moss

Animal: Cow

Elements: Fire

Energy: Healing, raw primal power, organic structuring, vital forces, manifestation, survival, and quintessential patterning

Magical Uses: Self-care, personal space, courage, rites of passage, health and wellness, freedom, creativity, inspiration, independence, and freedom.

Divinations: Vitality, pattern, tenacity, strength, luck, constancy, practical knowledge, understanding, OR inconstancy, ignorance, weakness, insensitivity, misdirected rage, sickness, and brutality.

| 1 | 2 | 3 |

Three Norns Method ᚱ ᛁ ᛈ

The Three Norns Method in Norse mythology is named after the three goddesses of fate. It requires picking three runes in exactly the same way as you do for the one-rune method. Place the three runes side by side (see diagram above) and read them in the order they were drawn. The reading is specific to the past, present, and future and is read from right to left.

Position 1: URD placement: reveals situations in the past that are directly related to the present and are setting the groundwork for the future.

Position 2. Verdandi placement: reveals present situations and will point out any decisions that you are going to have to make very soon.

Position 3. Skuld placement: reveals a veiled future, with parts unknown. It may show you the outcome of a present dilemma or provide you with a potential future scenario that depends on your choices in life.

Scrying

Historically, scrying has been characterized by the image of a fortune teller peering into her crystal ball. This has been used a lot in a negative way. However, scrying, like all arcane practices, is not about telling fortunes or "seeing your future." The future can only be theorized based on the information you have at the present moment. The word "scrying" is rooted in the Old English word "descry" which means to reveal or to "dimly make out." Hence, scrying references what is unseen by using our innate second sight. Our "second sight" is our ability to see aspects that usually cannot be distinguished through our five senses. Once the technique is understood, you will be able to connect to your unconscious mind. Therefore, it can be a powerful way to understand yourself. If you are having a hard time finding direction, purpose, and meaning in your life, scrying is a beautiful and amazing way to connect with your goals, dreams, and essential needs.

Scrying is usually performed by using a crystal ball, mirror, water, or another reflective surface. However, it is important to note that there are many other techniques. The other common techniques are:

1. Wax: The practitioner drips wax onto the surface of water. The scryer then analyzes and interprets the words or images created from the wax that has dried on the surface of the water.
2. Mirror: This is a very well-known scrying technique. Also known as catoptromancy, this method is conducted by putting yourself in a relaxed state, further relaxing your eyes, and gazing into a mirror. It doesn't take long for scenes and images to emerge.
3. Water: Using the same technique as with mirror scrying, only gazing into a pool or body of water. Some scryers may drop a pebble into the water to read the ripples that are created.

4. Cloud: Cloud gazing is a technique whereby you observe and analyze the shapes formed by clouds. This is a special form of information gathering.
5. Oil: This is done by rubbing oil on your body, pouring some into a dish, or coating a plate or cup with oil. The scryer then pays attention to the way the light is reflected off of the oiled object for interpretation.
6. Fire: This is the oldest form of scrying and is accomplished by experiencing visions while staring into fiery flames. You can do this with an oil lamp or candle, but bonfires are magically powered for this technique.
7. Crystal: This is the crystal ball technique. Many different types of crystals are used to create magical and beautiful globes for effective readings of special meaning.
8. Smoke: Watching smoke rising from a fire creates ethereal images that provide you with spiritual information.
9. Eye: This is the most unusual! Also referred to as soul gazing, this scrying technique involves staring deeply into the eyes of a person and interpreting the reflections you see.

Water Scrying Method

Here is a water lesson for your enjoyment and to give you a starting point if you don't already have one. You're welcome to copy this technique or create your own. Also, don't feel restricted to this type of water scrying, especially if you don't feel drawn to it. Practice with the variety of techniques for scrying I described above.

Materials

- 1 Black bowl
- Moon water or blessed water (you can use purified water or collect rainwater; even better)
- 2 Black candles
- Lighter
- Clear quartz crystal
- Table
- Sage bundle or incense

Steps

1. Dark bowls help you to focus better. Fill your bowl with one of the water recipes or use bottled water.
2. Prepare your sacred space. You can be inside or outside, but you want to be in the dark. Smudge the area.

3. Place your clear quartz crystal in the center of the bowl. Clear quartz balances and amplifies your intentions. Make sure to center your crystal because it will be the focal point for your eyes.
4. Place your candles on each side of your bowl and light them.
5. Enter your meditation and transform yourself into a trance-like state. When you are in a trance, your state of consciousness is altered. Just about every culture in the world has trance rituals; some involve chanting, fasting, beating a drum, and dancing. I personally always do a deep breathing exercise.
6. Once you have entered your trance, begin to gaze into the bowl. You will know when you're ready because, in an altered state, you will feel connected, peaceful, alert, focused, and expanded. If you don't feel these emotions, take more time.
7. Most of all, relax your eyes and focus on your crystal. Water scrying can take practice to master, so be patient.
8. With your intention strong in your mind, let your eyes and your entire face relax and breathe deeply.
9. You can allow your vision to soften as images may start to come and go. Don't try

to make them stay. Allow them to flow, coming and going freely, while feeling their sensations. You want to passively observe the images. This takes practice.

10. After a moment or two, you will feel your mind starting to wander. Allow this to happen. Be sure to keep your eyes focused on the water.
11. It is normal for an image or a whole scene to play out before your very eyes.
12. Once you feel you have the answers, you may want to meditate on the scenes, words, or images you have experienced.
13. Ask yourself what they were attempting to reveal to you. Sometimes, it will be extremely evident, and other times, not so much. So, look out for metaphors, analogies, and symbols that may carry a meaning close to your intention.

Pendulum Dowsing

One of the most popular divination techniques is pendulum dowsing. A pendulum (see image above) is a weighted object, symmetrical in shape, and usually crystal in composition. Some may use beads, a metal ball, their sacred trinket, or even a key. It never is made of material that is magnetic. The pendulum works to receive and transmit information, and shifts direction differently in response to the questions. Pendulum dowsing can help you with making decisions, answer your questions as well as other magical uses:

- Identify a person's allergies and other healing purposes.
- To dispel negative vibrations and cleanse a sacred space.
- To assist you in finding your lost pet or a lost object.
- To point you in the direction of water.

How Pendulum Dowsing Works

Pendulum dowsing taps into your sense and intuition. The pendulum functions to receive and transmit information between your spiritual advisors and guardian angels—your higher power. As it sways, the answers to your questions will come to you. "Yes" and "no" questions are the easiest to read. Dowsing actually connects your left and right sides of the brain, which are the intuitive and logical sides of you. When those two elements are connected, you can come to decisions using all of your resources, rather than only one of them. Like all forms of magic, your intentions, faith, and beliefs are necessary for competent readings. Most commonly, dowsers use clear quartz but you only need to put the keyword "pendulum dowsing" in any search engine to see hundreds of crystal species used for dowsing. Again, use what you are drawn to or spend some time researching the many beautiful properties of crystals. The crystal you choose has to be pointed or rounded on one end. Here are some steps to follow:

1. Smudge or cleanse and charge your pendulum with any of the methods discussed in this book. Sun charging, catching the sun's rays, is also a great idea.
2. Keep it in a safe place, such as a velvet pouch or a silk wrap.
3. Put all of your doubts aside and come in with an open mind.
4. Hold the string or cord of the pendulum in whichever hand feels most comfortable, between your forefinger and your thumb.
5. If the cord feels too long, wrap it around your finger. Some pendulums come with a small ring at the top that can be held.
6. Sit comfortably with the cord of your pendulum between your thumb and

forefinger. Using your other hand, run down the length of the cord, bringing your hand so it is resting with the tip of the bottom of the pendulum in your palm, facing up.
7. Now the pendulum is completely still and you can gently move away your hand from its bottom.
8. It is completely normal for the pendulum to start moving.
9. Continuing to stay relaxed watch the movement of the pendulum.
10. After a few moments, give "yes" and "no" questions a go, either aloud or in your mind.
11. Be patient when waiting for your answer. At first, ask simple questions, as it takes time to create a relationship with your pendulum and know how you both interact.
12. Practice by asking your pendulum to show you "yes" and "no" responses until you come to a full understanding of the different motions.
13. Some pendulums, when answering "yes" swing in a wide circular motion that can change with time. If anyone touches your pendulum other than you, it will need to be cleansed and recharged with your unique energy.

14. As you become familiar with responses, you can gradually begin to inquire about personal decisions that you are making in your life.
15. You can also hold your pendulum over a map and ask it to find something you are searching for, such as a lost pet or connection.

The Futhark Runes

RUNE	NAME	TRANSLATION	MEANING
ᚠ	Fehu	F	Prosperity, wealth, fulfilment, cattle, gain
ᚢ	Uruz	U	Determination, wild ox, life force, strength
ᚦ	Thurisaz	Th	Thor, unexpected changes, giants, brutal force
ᚨ	Ansuz	A	Odin, communication, mouth, transferring of information

ᚱ	Raido	R	Travel, journey, introspection, movement, wagon
ᚲ	Kaunaz	C/K	Energy, positive attitude, fire, power, warmth
ᚷ	Gebo	G	Partnership, gift, serendipitous outcome, commitment
ᚹ	Wunjo	W	Lasting happiness, emotional joy, success
ᚺ	Hagalaz	H	Disruption, hail, limitations, forces beyond your control
ᚾ	Nauthiz	N	Hardship, patience, need, learning through hardship
ᛁ	Isa	I	Ice, frustrations, putting your plans on hold

	Jera	J/Y	Justice, harvest, rewards for past efforts
	Eihwaz	E	Resilience, endurance, Yew, goal achievement, Yggdrasil (a friend of the clear blue sky)
	Pertho	P	Randomness, secrets uncovered, mystery, coincidence, knowledge of the occult

FINAL THOUGHTS

I hope you have enjoyed this detailed narrative about the world of witchcraft rituals, white, red, black, and rune magic with this step-by-step guide to spell casting, rune reading, and the many other concepts of magic that we have described. With this book of magical spells you should be able to sharpen your skills and set your intentions with techniques and methods that will nourish you and guide you to where you want to go as an experienced witch. I hope that I have added some incredible new spells to your magic repertoire. At this point, you have hopefully learned the techniques associated with white, red and black magic, runes, and divinations; how to conduct the ritual of calling quarters and candle magic. Interpreting runes will be ever so much easier to understand after reviewing the material outlined in this book. By reading this book you have hopefully learned how to cast a circle, cleanse your sacred space, what colors represent in the world of magic, how to call upon the elements, and so much more.

I have shared my skill set and in-depth understanding and education about casting spells and the Wiccan culture. Your life will be passionately transformed through enlightenment and spiritual connectedness.

The history of runes was explained to provide an interpretation guide for the beginner witch. Various rituals, spells, and methods, including poppet construction, scrying, pendulum dowsing, and others were outlined; you can incorporate them into your life on a daily basis and create a magical environment in which your spells can be manifested. Each spell described how to communicate your intentions by using your intuition to interpret findings and discover the worlds beyond our own. Natural potions and crystal magic are a huge component of practicing witchcraft and Wiccans have been doing the research on them for centuries.

Understanding the importance of dispelling myths about Hoodoo and black magic is a responsibility witches should share. The racist undertones are relevant in today's turbulent and trying times. People undeniably have associated black witches with black magic and other magical deeds trumped up in the media as harmful and dangerous. Historically, black witches have mainly been portrayed as evil and as only practicing hoodoo, voodoo, or other forms of stigmatized magic.

Hopefully, you gained a keen understanding of the importance of herbs and essential oils as integral components to magic. A spell or a potion is only as good as its ingredients. Many individuals have come to use essential oils and herbal remedies for balancing and unblocking the chakras, with specific herbs and specific oils offering different properties for each chakra. Both oils and herbs are used to access information from the spiritual realm and our subconscious and unconscious minds. By using essential oils and essential herbs in our magical practices, we can direct very specific energies towards our intentions for healing, personal growth, and other spells and rituals, of which there are too many to name. They are so powerful that they work outside of our conscious will.

"I hope you enjoy this book as much as I loved writing it. If you do, it would be wonderful if you could take a short minute and leave a review on Amazon as soon as you can, as your kind feedback is much appreciated and so very important. Thank you."

SOURCES

Ezzy, D. (2006). White witches and black magic: Ethics and consumerism in contemporary witchcraft. *Journal of Contemporary Religion* 21(1)15-31. Print.

Greenwood, S. (2015). The anthropology of magic. *Oxford: Berg*. Print.

Magic, Witchcraft and the Otherworld: An Anthropology. *Bloomsbury Academic*. 2000. Print.

Jensen, G. & Thompson, A. (2008). Out of the broom closet: The social ecology of American Wicca. *Journal for the Scientific Study of Religion* 47(4) 753-66. Print.

"magic, n." OED Online, *Oxford University Press*, March 2019

Manning, M. (2014). [Introduction]: Magic, religion, and ritual in historical archaeology. *Historical Archaeology* 48(3)1-9. Print.

Styers, R. (2012). Mana and mystification: Magic and religion at the turn of the twentieth century. *Women's Studies Quarterly 40*.(¾) 226–43. Print.

www.ingramcontent.com/pod-product-compliance
Lightning Source LLC
Chambersburg PA
CBHW021437070526
44577CB00002B/201